TWO MORE YEARS

A Memoir by
EC STILSON

TWO MORE YEARS
Copyright © 2022 by EC Stilson

FIRST EDITION SOFTCOVER
ISBN: 1622537815
ISBN-13: 978-1-62253-781-5

Editor: Robb Grindstaff
Cover Artist: Kris Norris
Interior Designer: Lane Diamond
Cover Photo: Mike Magagna
Wing Painting on Cover Photo: Art By Rainee
Tattoo Art on Cover: Ruby Morris

EVOLVED PUBLISHING™
www.EvolvedPub.com
Evolved Publishing LLC
Butler, Wisconsin, USA

Two More Years a narrative memoir, in which some of the names
have been changed to protect certain individuals' privacy.
Nonetheless, events depicted here are true, at least according to the
author's memory and perspective, with any memory gaps filled in
realistically in an appropriate manner.

Printed in Book Antiqua font.

BOOKS BY EC STILSON

NOVELS AND MEMOIRS
A Stranger's Kindness
Best of EC Writes
Bible Girl
Homeless in Hawaii
One Wing in the Fire
The Golden Sky
The Sword of Senack
Two More Years

NOVELLAS
How to Avoid Having Sex
Threaded Dreams

CHILDREN'S BOOKS
How to Lose a Tooth
The Smallest Peach

SHORT STORIES
(EC Stilson's stories have appeared in the following anthologies.)
Christmas Lites I
Christmas Lites II
Fractured Fairytales
Frightening Fairytales
My Funny Major Medical
Open Doors I
Open Doors II

For photos and videos from *TWO MORE YEARS*, go to:
www.TwoMoreYears.net

WHAT OTHERS ARE SAYING

"EC Stilson's cancer memoir is so beautifully written, inspiring, and poignant. The words shine hope into the darkest days." ~ *Eileen Wharton, Writer of Crime Novels, Women's Fiction, and Children's Books*

"EC Stilson's story might not be unique, but her voice is. If anything, it's the universality of her struggle that makes her words worth reading. She brings a light and observant deftness to her prose that belies the severity of her survival. When you read Stilson, you learn that existence is a human condition; it's how we live, how we love, how we laugh, and learn to live within the bedlam we've created that gives us our actual humanity." ~ *Nick Bruel, Author of the "Bad Kitty" Series*

"EC Stilson has been a daily source of inspiration to people of every age and from all walks of life... particularly those facing life's most difficult challenges." ~ *Loree Lough, USA Today Bestselling Author of 140 Award-Winning Books*

"EC Stilson has been a source of inspiration to me. Her attitude of gratitude is infectious, and her courage to share her walk with others comes through in every one of her stories." ~ *Mark Gabriel, Managing Director and Owner/Principal Investor of G2 Productions*

~~~

"EC Stilson shares her profoundly uplifting personal journey from the lowest depths of despair and the insurmountable adversity of cancer to the triumph of unconditional love and an unquenchable thirst for life." ~ *Joanna Lee Doster, Author of "Tails of Jaxx," A Children's Mystery Series*

"I have never met EC Stilson in person, but I feel that I know her well enough to feel like she's a close friend. I have read her stories posted on social media for what seems like years and always find them heartfelt, touching, and sometimes funny. And yes, she's made me cry on more than one occasion. She's given me hope that I can overcome my own relatively minor ailments with dignity and a positive outlook." ~ *William Vaughn, Author of "The Seldith Chronicles"*

"Some of Stilson's posts have brought me to tears—and this is coming from a fellow writer. She is so brave in the face of pain and the unknown yet manages to be positive and kind. I am rooting for her and hope she lives a good, long life." ~ *Marya Ashworth, Author of "The Elven Chronicles"*

"I am an avid reader of Stilson's and feel inspired most of all by her sense of balance with regard to honestly reporting about her difficulties, but at the same time finding moments of joy, love, and gratitude within it all. The camera loves her face, and her readers love her thoughts." ~ *Anthony Flacco, Author of "The Last Nightingale" Historical Crime Series*

And many, many more, which you can find
starting at this page:
www.EvolvedPub.com/ECStilson.

DEDICATION

For Mike and our children: Ruby, Sky, Trey, and Indiana.

*Your courage and strength through this entire
journey are inspiring.*

You amaze me.

CHAPTER 1
Two Years

Several doctors couldn't pinpoint the root of my issues. "I'm not calling you a liar," a specialist said. "I'm just saying we can't find anything wrong with you. Without other evidence, there's no way your insurance will pay for an MRI."

Without answers, the doubts and worries crept in. Would this just go away some day, as suddenly as it had come on? I could barely walk, feeling crippled. What if I died from a strange malady that could only be found in an autopsy? Why couldn't the "experts" help me?

Where was Dr. House when I needed him?

I mulled mortality, wondering what my purpose has been. Raising my kids, yes. But beyond that? Writing has always been an integral part of my life. I'd been a newspaper publisher. Written two memoirs and several novels, some of which met with decent success. Music, playing the violin, is a key part of who I am.

Feeling like my last lifeline hung, severed, I got an unexpected text:

She wanted you to have this.

The words brought me to a time before, when I ran a little newspaper in Blackfoot, Idaho, and wrote opinion pieces about the amazing people in town. I'd been vivacious and fun — not this shadow of myself.

While there, I briefly met a woman named Norma Furniss. Even the first time I saw her, she shone with an unforgettable intensity. Her eyes saw much more than they should have, and she carried a wisdom befitting her ninety-six years. Ever-changing like time, it appeared she'd outlive us all — and maybe that's why her death surprised me. Yet, months later her wishes lived on, and I got that message from her son, Nolan.

He came to my house after that, and when he walked from his vehicle with that Quiet Riter — the same typewriter Norma herself had used — well, I couldn't hold back my joy. I hugged him, telling him how much it meant to me.

That night, my husband cleared a special place on my writing desk where he set up the typewriter. And there it rested, waiting....

***

"I give you two years to live."

A few months after they couldn't find the root of my issues, hospitalized again, I sat facing yet another doctor — an oncologist.

My heart froze in time at the dreaded words. To not see my kids grow up, start their careers, get married. To not grow old with Mike. Unfathomable thoughts.

"I'm only thirty-seven. You can fix this. Can't you?" I'd made so many plans.

"I'm sorry, Elisa. We can't."

Stage four melanoma. It had spread to my spine and brain. My breath evaded me, like I already needed the ventilator — the damn life support.

He told me they'd slated a surgery. It wasn't to prolong my life; it was just to help abate the pain.

After he left, I ordered a hospital smoothie, looked out the window, and tried to pretend I was in Puerto Vallarta. Salt Lake doesn't *really* look like Mexico, but if you imagine long enough, you can almost see crocodiles and an ocean in the distance!

Mike came to visit, but I didn't tell him what the surgeon said. Every time I tried, my voice broke on the words. He ended up doing my hair in a fancy braid, just to take my mind from things.

"Oh!" I said. "I forgot to tell you. A nurse saw me crying in my room today."

"You were crying?"

"Yeah, but that's not the good part. She let me play my violin in the lobby because she felt so bad."

Mike laughed. "Really?"

It was a captive audience. Why would I ever pass that up?

"They brought patients from all over the different floors. Seriously though, I think it helped me more than it helped them. I met a guy about my age. He's been battling for a few years, and he's starting to improve." I swallowed hard. "I could get better... someday too. Maybe."

"Of course, you will," Mike said, but his big eyes filled with concern as he gazed out the window. Maybe he wished we could be away from this place — maybe he wanted to be in Puerto Vallarta too.

Some hope did remain, in surgeries and immunotherapy, but despite that, they said cancer would cut my life short. At only thirty-seven years old, I'd need to get my affairs in order and draft a will.

Back home again, I sat at my writing desk in front of the old typewriter, Norma's Quiet Riter. To keep from crying, I imagined Norma from years ago, sitting in front of that same typewriter. The machine is nearly seventy years old. She must have owned it early in her marriage. What amazing stories had she written on this ancient machine?

Maybe I didn't really know my purpose. Maybe none of us do. Writing had always been a part of my life, but was my purpose on this earth to raise a family and write a few books?

I will never forget Norma or her kindness, even after her death. Maybe my words could be like that for others. After all, we're all human, just trying to get through this mess called life.

But the old typewriter sat there, unmoving, staring at me, silent. Why did Norma leave this to me? She must have seen something more in me.

I rested my fingers in the home typing position. As I touched the keys, courage flowed into me.

The typewriter wasn't a symbol that I was supposed to be a great or famous writer, but a reminder that I'm supposed to share my journey. To write about my experiences with cancer, the good and the bad. Maybe my failures and triumphs will help others, so they don't feel so alone.

So I won't feel alone.

CHAPTER 2
Brain Radiation

Getting through two-hour MRIs and extended CTs has become easier with months of practice: I meditate and count. I even imagine I'm at a spa that offers me a wrinkle-free forehead and beautifully tanned skin. But as I prepared for the brain tumor radiation, no amount of pretending calmed me.

"I'll be right here in the waiting room," Mike said.

"Okay!" I feigned strength.

The techs led me into a room with all sorts of large whirring machines and flashing screens. A specialist told me to remove my hospital gown. "But I'm only wearing a pair of panties...." And to my horror I remembered which pair I'd worn! Mike had bought me a new pack of underwear after I got admitted to the hospital, and apparently men go for fashion over comfort.

"We see people in their underwear every day," a woman said.

I reluctantly handed them my gown and stood there in my sparkly slut underwear. At least my fake boobs didn't look bad, but the underwear cast little lights on the wall as if we were in a strip club instead of a cancer center.

It took a minute to wriggle into what they called my nest.

"Sorry," I apologized. "My back still hurts so much from where they removed the tumor."

"You'll feel better once you get in there. It's an exact mold we took of your body."

Soon I rested horizontally in the sarcophagus-thing, and they placed washcloths over my shivering breasts and pushed the sides of the cast against my arms until my wedding ring dug into my thigh. "I forgot to take off my wedding ring!"

"No worries. We're not radiating that area anyway." A woman grabbed some straps and began tying me down.

"Wait. What are you doing?" Each of my breaths shortened as *Streetcar Named Desire* popped into my head.

"Radiation is extremely powerful. We can't have even the slightest movement. We're radiating very specific spots in your back and brain, but if we hit the wrong areas — especially in your cerebrum — well, that could be devastating."

I smelled something putridly metallic, and my vision blurred. I wondered if the anti-anxiety medication had caused these additional symptoms. "Can you tell me a story — to distract me?"

"Um, sure. So, we had a biker guy come in a few weeks ago. He promised not to move. We all would've bet on him, but during radiation he flipped out, actually getting out of the restraints, ripping the plastic cage off his face, and damaging part of the machine! So, don't feel bad if you're a little nervous. It can happen to anyone — even a burly biker guy."

Well, great. I tried lengthening my breaths, but nothing seemed to help. "I can't believe how nervous I am. I bet this wouldn't even phase my husband." Then

I told them all about Mike and what a strong person he is.

"All right." They patted the cast above my shoulder. "We're almost ready. Just hang weightless. We'll do the rest." Two sets of hands lifted my head and placed it into a cradle that wrapped uncomfortably tight against my ears.

"This will keep your throat open." They pointed to a plastic mouthpiece protruding from the inside of the mask. "Bite down on this when we put the mask on."

Then the worst part—the face mask felt so confining I couldn't open my eyes. It squished my nose and pressed the plastic far into my mouth until saliva pooled near the back of my teeth.

"We have to bolt you to the table—it's protocol. Just relax."

Something whirred near my ear; it sounded suspiciously like a screwdriver.

That's when my mind went wild. Every horror show I've ever seen came to mind. Could I trust these people? Was this even a real hospital? What if they radiated the wrong part of my brain, and I turned into a genuine asshole?

"Mmm!" I tried yelling—because I *did not* want to be an asshole.

They didn't respond.

My arms and legs remained mummified—immobile and weak.

"Mmm...."

Suddenly, I remembered caving with Mike years before. I'd gotten stuck, and I didn't think I could wriggle free. Darkness enveloped me along with a strange coldness that took hold as rocks dug deeper and deeper into my skin. Time suspended as I struggled like a worm, trying to wrestle my way to freedom. That's how I felt as they bolted me to the table.

I tried to thump my body, but like a Chinese finger trap, the weight and pressure of the mold intensified, getting warmer and tighter as it shrunk around me.

The techs' footsteps faded away. They'd left me all alone.

I tried one last time, my breathing so labored I thought I might pass out. And as my arm stretched, the mold crunched slightly to my right.

"Wait! I think she's freaking out," a tech said from the end of the room. "Are you okay?" He raised his voice.

"Nnn — ttt! Nnn — ttt!" Fiery tears streamed from the sides of my eyes and into the face mask as I bit down even harder on the plastic in my mouth.

The tech barked urgent orders before the screwdriver whirred once more, and the radiation team removed the mask.

My lips quivered. "I can't do this! I can't!" My voice rose to a ridiculous level.

"It's just fifty minutes."

"That's almost an hour! I'm freaking out. Get me out of this."

"Listen, Elisa. You have two brain tumors — one malignant and one benign. We have to do this, or the cancer will spread in your brain. You have no chance without radiation. No. Chance. Don't you want more time with your kids and your husband?"

I understood. "I know I need to do this, but —" I bawled. "I just can't get through it. I feel like I'm getting buried alive or something."

"Wait," a tech said. "You heard her talking about her husband. We need to go get him."

Mike rushed in mere moments later. "Hey. Hey. You're okay," he said.

His face betrayed his shock at seeing what radiation entailed. I'd been embarrassed enough for him to see me with my shaved head the day before—but now this.

As if reading my thoughts, he placed a reassuring hand on my forehead. "You're gonna be okay. Don't worry. I have an idea."

I nodded and bit my lip.

"Close your eyes, Elisa."

I breathed in, shut my eyes, and listened to his voice.

"Okay. I need you to imagine you're a violin."

I hung onto his every word. As his deep voice relayed minute details about what I should visualize, his love encased me instead of the body mold. The intense heat seemed fueled from the passion in his tone and the lights fully embodied his belief in me.

"You're getting fixed up right now. They're going to shine up your wooden surfaces. Work on each part."

The techs gently inserted the mouthpiece and pressed the mask against my face.

"They're polishing and refining you, tuning your strings, adjusting your bridge."

I breathed strong, steady breaths.

"You're just going to get fixed up a bit. You're a violin."

"We need to step out now," a tech said after screwing the mask back in place. "She's quiet this time. She seems okay."

The table slid, rocking me as it jostled. More lights bored forward, penetrating even the face cage and my closed eyelids.

I imagined that God inspected every part of a violin. The heavy encasings around my legs buffed my surfaces and stained my edges. God would come so I could be perfected, cleansed, and refined.

A violin maker had asked to borrow my fiddle years before. I reluctantly gave it to him, not having any idea why he wanted it. Over a matter of days, he'd done all sorts of wonderful things: sanding and rehairing, rebuilding, painting, and retuning. He gave me a new chin rest and bridge! My violin gleamed from the beauty of his intentions, and I'd hugged him tightly for doing such a wonderful act of kindness. My violin sang like never before.

As the minutes ticked by, I truly felt what my violin must have undergone. And when the radiation machine stopped, I somehow embodied peace.

Mike's voice echoed off the walls as he rushed into the room. "You're done! You did it!"

When they removed the mask, a man asked Mike, "How did you think of that? How? It was brilliant, really."

"I don't know. It just came to me."

I opened my eyes and stared at my husband's handsome face. "Thank you for helping me!"

"You're so brave." He smiled, and somehow hearing him say those words meant more to me than anything in the world.

I'll continue coming back for radiation on my spine. I hope I'll get better at this.

***

Another time, another place, many years ago, I'm lying on my back, practically shining with happiness.

My chubby toes twiddle in front of me, and I'm purely delighted that I can tell my body to move, and then it magically obeys.

So much joy. The creatures in the fish tank behind me move and dance in a strange world all their own. I love the betta fish best because they seem to wear flowing dresses that fit just perfectly!

There's a bay window in front of me. And the sunlight catches all sorts of dust particles. I let my feet playfully fall to the carpet, and that's when I take my hands out of my mouth and start trying to grab the tiny flecks that are illuminated all around.

It's magic—my first memory. I'm so filled with wonder and joy, enough that it lasted a lifetime.

I loved everything to the fullest: those around me, the beauty of simplicity, even the warmth of the sun. It's strange to think that the sun eventually made me so sick. What inspired my first memory might also be the cause of my last. It's not a shock really; after all, it's far more common for people with reddish hair to get melanoma. And looking back, it doesn't matter so much. Not anymore. It's too late.

The sun made an impact so strong that it's my first memory—that and a pure joy of just being alive. I've heard that first memories can give us a glimpse into our purpose. Well, I'd say mine is joy, experiencing it and then trying to share it with others. It's that simple.

***

> *Dear God,*
> *I think I've handled things fairly well (except for the face-cage radiation). I've laughed when I should've cried, been nice when I*

could've screamed about my mortality. Tried to be brave. And I've really handled it well, until the extended butt crack.

I decided to look at my scar, which goes from the middle of my back down to my tailbone. But no matter which light it's in — trust me — the scar now makes my butt crack look a million miles long, and it's not even in the right place! Cheeks extending between my shoulder blades is not what I asked for this Christmas.

When Sir Mix-a-Lot wrote about liking big butts, I don't think he meant the hunch-butt of Notre Dame. But still, if I'm trying to be positive, I finally have a big butt, and if I had to get a weird thing for Christmas 2020, a lifesaving surgery is pretty great. The worst side effect was, simply, a back butt.

It's a good thing my daughter, Ruby, is training to be a tattoo artist. I've never wanted a tattoo in my life, but I might need one to cover up the scar. It's funny how life will change us.

Sincerely,

A woman with a back butt

PS: Don't ever get cancer. It comes with all sorts of things that no one wants.

CHAPTER 3
My Demise Cheered Them

The radiation waiting room is a strange place where everyone wears patient gowns, and no one really checks in—yet we're all recognized and called back in order.

I hobbled in with my walker. This wasn't a regular day though, and the air felt thick. Two elderly women sat bickering about life, even though they seemed relatively rich, well-to-do (from their hair, nails, and conversation), and as if they've lacked nothing their entire lives.

"Why did God *do* this to us?" one woman asked. "This is the most terrible thing I can imagine."

"I agree! I might stop going to church. This is ridiculous!"

They both complained so long it grated against my nerves more than my back surgery. They talked about how they both have breast cancer (stage one and stage two). Radiation for both is precautionary, and they have good prognoses ahead of them. I thought they were actually quite lucky, yet they complained.

"Don't ever get old!" one lady said to me. "It's the pits."

But, oddly enough, I was there—getting radiation— to get old.

"Getting old sucks," she said.

And I wanted to follow with, "No, dying young sucks." Instead, I looked at the TV and hoped one of them would be called back soon before I said something I'd regret.

But they weren't, and the older of the two sighed deeply. "I'm sure it's something simple, but what are you in here for?" she asked me.

I couldn't take it anymore. She wanted answers. Then, fine! "Stage four melanoma. They've given me two years to live."

You should've seen their faces — the older one looked like she'd swallowed a frog. The other woman lost some of the color in her plump face. And I don't know why, but this must have worked as some sort of reset. They started apologizing as I held in some devious laughter.

"And here we are, talking about how hard *our* lives are."

"We all die sometime," I said. "And that's hard for everyone. We just need to start appreciating the time while we're here. Why complain when you could be enjoying life? One is a waste, and the other isn't."

After a few minutes of silence, the two started talking about how lucky they were not to have stage four cancer, and how they have upcoming plans for the holidays — gifts for family and friends. They talked about a future far beyond that, one I hope they'll have. And as each of them was called back to radiation, they smiled and told me to never lose hope. It felt odd, how my demise had cheered them up. But honestly, I was grateful something had done the trick.

A new lady sat in the room with me at that point. She seemed sweet despite circumstances. And I thought how amusing that she hadn't seen what had transpired in that same room, just moments before.

***

A few days later, we went to Walmart to get a couple of dollar gifts for each of the kids—just to tell them we appreciate how well they're handling everything. But several minutes into the trip, I started feeling weak and dizzy. I looked frantically for a place to sit, but COVID had wiped out all the chairs.

I finally hobbled to the front of the store and found a seat where an associate had previously been peddling eyewear. I know it probably isn't right, but as soon as they stood, I sat down as if we were playing a game of musical chairs. With my walker in front of me, I hoped no one would argue about the place I'd illegally commandeered.

I sat, staring to the left when someone said something directly to my right. I looked over, shocked. A man perched not six feet away. I had no idea where he had found his chair, but I wasn't about to judge him when I'd just done the same.

"You use this thing?" he asked, softly kicking my walker.

Who was this guy? "Yes," I said, trying to be extra polite. "I use this thing."

"Well then, what's wrong with you? You're not *that* old."

"I'm in my thirties." Had he seriously just asked what's wrong with me? This man was so blunt, and part of me loved it

"I have cancer," I admitted. "Stage four." It felt nice to get it out. A lot of people in the store had looked at me like they wondered what's wrong but weren't brave enough to ask.

The man leaned forward then, as if imparting some great gift. "The reason I'm here is to tell you that prayer works."

"That's the reason you're here?"

"Yep. That's the reason I'm here!" I could tell he smiled under his mask.

Shortly after that, Mike came up to a register, and I went to stand by him as he checked out.

As we walked away, I looked back to where I'd been sitting. The chairs were gone. So was the man I'd spoken with moments before.

"Who was that?" Mike asked.

"I have no idea. But that was one of the weirdest things I've had happen in weeks. And that's saying something."

"What did he say?"

"That prayer works."

We went out to the car, set the tiny bag of dollar gifts in the backseat, and drove off.

I shook my head as we traveled along. I just couldn't stop thinking about that strange man and his timely message.

***

You can watch some pretty great things on the TV in the radiation waiting room, depending on the time you get there. First thing in the morning is the news, then *Charmed* (of all things), yuppie sitcoms, and later in the day we watch The Cooking Channel.

During another cooking contest, I wondered how many times they'd feature duck or goose. About ten other people waited with me, and everybody seemed somber. You never know what it'll be like in the waiting room — the emotional temperature totally changes depending on the people.

Anyway, I'm not quite sure why, but a seed of excitement sprouted inside of me, and I suddenly decided to make a difference. We were all in there because of cancer, obviously miserable. We're not even allowed to have our cellphones. Somehow, I could make this fun.

We all listened to the TV. "This is the worst duck I've ever tasted," the woman said. "In fact, I can't think of anything worse than this duck."

"Try cancer," I said out of nowhere. "Cancer is *way* worse than that duck."

Everyone in the waiting room turned to me.

"And this sauce, few things are worse than this sauce."

A man next to me burst out laughing and said, "But cancer, cancer is worse than that sauce."

I don't know why, but it became the most hilarious moment. As the cooking show continued, everyone laughed and laughed. It was as if the whole thing had been orchestrated perfectly for the most hilarious comedy session—right there in the radiation waiting room.

Finally, a nurse called my name.

"Oh, no! You no take her," a lady said with a gorgeous accent. "She's the light of the party."

I smiled so broadly and turned to everyone before I left. "Best of everything—to all of you."

And I thanked God for a rare moment that was so beautiful, a moment where we could enjoy each other and our time despite sickness or differences... or anything really.

That moment was a true gift.

CHAPTER 4
A Generous Community

I was done with the first sets of radiation! Now for infusions (immunotherapy) every six weeks and scans every third therapy. I still only had a two-year prognosis, but nothing could get me down. We were finally home in Idaho—and not just for the weekend. I was so happy to be with my kids, enjoying life as much as I could.

I couldn't believe what waited for us when we got home. It felt like the entire community rallied around to offer support. We received dozens of packages in the mail: blankets, care kits, hats, wigs, gloves. Indy's elementary school even dropped off a ton of food this afternoon from neighbors who had cooked numerous meals. We even got tacos!

I cried when I read a note from a stranger. "Happy holidays! You are all in our hearts. Stay strong, Elisa."

I hate having cancer, but I was so grateful my kids saw how kindness can change lives. There must be a huge reason we're going through all of this. I'm learning so much about people, who I want to be, and how I want to respond to hardship. How will this impact the kind of adults my kids become?

***

My mother is fancy, wielding a class even Grace Kelly would envy. She came all the way from Arizona to help take care of me, and I was excited when she asked me out to dinner.

I rummaged through my best clothes, donned my fake eyelashes, and delicately placed a headband over the main bald spot where I've lost hair from radiation.

"You know," my mom whispered in the fancy restaurant, "that's the owner over there. I've always wanted to meet him. I've heard he knows some people I grew up with."

And taking this as some sort of challenge, I looked at the man and said, "Are you from Price?"

"No, I'm from Greece."

He hadn't really understood me at all, so my mom stepped in. "What she means is, do you know people from Price, Utah? From Carbon County?"

He instantly lit up, and my mother and the owner of this fancy restaurant talked for quite a while about old friends and acquaintances. He even helped us at the register—a place where the hostess stepped aside so he could keep visiting.

I caught a reflection in the mirror behind the register. A woman with no hair, dilapidated walker in hand. Fading smile and dimming eyes. This woman hunched, with a frailty that made me want to hold her. She seemed so very, very sick. No long strawberry blond curls framing a youthful face.

Was that really me?

My rose-colored glasses shattered, and I realized how everyone—except my mother—looked at me.

The owner didn't look at me the way he would have months ago. You see, normally there's this odd brightness about me. It invites others to lighten their load and give into joy and fun—even for a minute. Somehow in that reflection, the brightness snuffed, and my own load became too great to carry.

The owner studied my walker. His eyes pried curiously, wanting to know what's wrong with me.

After that, my mom helped me hobble to the door, but the whole time, one sentence came to me, "You're not normal."

My mom—that saint—the whole way home told me how beautiful she thinks I am. Oohing and ahhing over my earrings and saying how my lack of hair brings out my gorgeous cheekbones. She didn't see that reflection, the one everyone in that restaurant saw.

"I'm gonna run to the bathroom," I said. By run, I meant trudge forward, back bent, legs shaking. After I made it to the bathroom, I quietly cried into the mirror, and I prayed God would get me through this. "God, keep me strong, and let me see myself through a mother's love." I wiped the makeup from under my eyes and told myself to quit being so weak. When I went outside, my mom had no idea what just happened. But I felt much better.

"Mom, can I put my head on your lap?"

She nodded, worried because I haven't done that since childhood. "Did you have a good night," she asked as I rested on her.

"Yeah," I said, "that was amazing how many of the same people you knew."

"Leave it to you, Elisa. I never would've known had it not been for you."

I smiled, then paused. "Thanks for loving me, Mom."

"Thanks for loving me back."

As I closed my eyes, I thought about reflections and how it's okay to not be strong all the time. If I could just have one day to feel healthy—really healthy again—I'd appreciate it! I'd hike, spin with my kids—anything really. I guess the saying is true: we don't always know what we have until it's gone.

***

We'd been so stressed about Christmas. I still worked remotely as an editor and Mike's work provided great health insurance, but bills piled up to a staggering amount.

Mike and I reluctantly told the kids that Christmas would be different this year. "We're renting a small cabin so we can play games. But each person will only get one gift."

Our ten-year-old's eyes grew big. "But Santa will come?"

I didn't realize Indy still believed.

My breath caught. "Sweetheart," I stooped down to her level, "I'm so sorry that I'm sick. You've had to be so strong while I was hospitalized. You've grown up much faster than you should've had to. And now this. There will just be one gift this year. I'm so sorry, Honey."

Tears filled her eyes as understanding about Santa suddenly hit. And I felt terrible for shattering her childhood magic like that. But then, Indy reached out, her little arms encircling me, gently touching where the incisions had been on my waist and back. "Mama, don't worry about any of that. Honestly, what I really wanted, I have. I just wanted you home. I wanted my mama back."

We held each other for a long time and cried.

I sat thinking about all of this when someone knocked on the front door. It was a sweet woman from Indy's school. She brought in six huge bags as my husband explained that we'd been picked to be the Angel Tree family.

"Wait, what?" I asked.

"While you stayed in the hospital, he filled out the forms," the woman said, beaming with such kindness.

I tried to keep my emotions at bay, but when she left, I had to sit down from the impact of the moment. They'd brought a bag for each child—and also a bag for me and for Mike.

I can't explain how hard it is to be in need like this, but I'm so happy for my little girl. I don't know who bought us these gifts, but they saved Christmas. I can hardly wait for Christmas next week.

***

Over a year before my diagnosis, I worked a staggering number of hours, hardly taking time for myself. Luckily, a certain dress shop felt like the perfect distraction from responsibilities, and the vintage clothes held so much magic, they could whisk anyone away.

I wandered through Annie Hall's store over a year ago. You can touch the fabric and practically feel the souls who wore the sets decades before. "Seeing" the past like that, well, there's nothing quite like it.

I continued, imagining what type of person had worn which set.

I ran a local newspaper and, after feeling the ambiance of the store, I vowed to somehow help the store's owner, Anne. We talked and she beamed, gushing about an upcoming fashion show where she'd help raise money to benefit people in need. She had no idea that I ran a paper or that *all* our readers would want to know about her kind endeavors.

I'd stayed up late editing photos and designing the page so it would look just perfect. I'll never forget Anne's bewilderment when I brought her a copy of the newspaper, and she saw one of her dresses on the front page. I'd completely baffled her.

"Next year, you'll be one of my models," she said, so elated.

I laughed because I'm in my late thirties and the girls in her show were young and perfect. "Oh, Anne!"

Then she grabbed a black velvet coat someone had just brought in. "I want you to try this on! Sometimes I just know what people are supposed to wear!" Then she vanished and reappeared with a matching black velvet dress. "Wear this dress with it."

It was an order, so I didn't argue. Anyone would be crazy to argue with Anne.

When I touched the dress, it felt like pure, living energy.

"That is a very special dress." Anne explained that it came complete with the original silk handkerchief that was about seventy years old.

Even though the price tag had it listed as one of the most expensive items in the store, I decided to try it on. The dress fit me like a second skin, zipping tightly in place, tailored to my exact shape.

"It's beautiful, isn't it?" Then Anne asked me to model it on the shop's rustic staircase, and she took so many pictures of me as I spun and grinned.

But even though I loved it, I could never afford such a dress. And no matter how much it had called to me, I placed it back on the hanger and left it displayed for the lucky rich woman who would inevitably buy it.

Time passed. Anne and I became friends, and the truth is, I fell for the sweet owner who makes everyone feel gorgeous.

Needless to say, 2020 came with hardships for everyone, but mine included cancer treatments, surgeries, and hair loss—and I didn't see Anne much anymore.

A few days before Christmas, Mike and I prepared to bring our kids to a cabin where we could make unforgettable memories. But my body felt extra worn, and I had to sit down.

"Are you feeling okay?" Mike asked, taking a break from packing.

"I'm struggling so much with self-esteem." I felt broken, unable to walk without my walker and feeling the flu-like symptoms that accompany treatments. I felt less than beautiful because I'd lost all of my hair.

It wasn't long after that when he said someone had FaceTimed us on the phone. Mike sauntered over, knowing I'd be happy to see Anne's face beaming on the screen.

"Anne!" I didn't know she even really knew Mike that well.

"This is from Anne," Mike said as he pulled something from behind his back.

The black velvet dress from 2019.

"It was meant for you," Anne said.

And then I cried.

My tears weren't just because of the gorgeous dress but because of Anne and her kindness. We've hit some pretty tough times but so many people like Anne have saved us and made things unfathomably better.

On Christmas Eve, I donned the dress, and as I looked in the mirror, I tried to stand as straight as I could. I smiled and for the first time in months I felt beautiful. I cried again, then went to the Christmas tree and sat in front of the lights.

We never know what the future will hold, but I'm awfully glad because it seems to be filled with such wonderful moments even in the darkest of times.

I could hardly wait for the kids to wake up in the morning and see the Angel Tree gifts. I'd be watching them while wearing the perfect Christmas dress from my Anne.

CHAPTER 5
Live Like You're Dyin'

Back before I knew I had cancer, one specific day the pain grew to such an intense level that I could hardly walk. I'd felt so frustrated, and a bit disheartened from my last visit to the doctor, because they'd told me this was "normal sciatic pain" and there was nothing they could do except send me to a chiropractor. My teenage daughters, Ruby and Sky, had confronted me, saying all I did was talk about myself and how much pain I felt. As their words replayed in my head, I really felt discredited.

After struggling to finish my remote work that day, I'd hobbled outside and decided to watch my younger kids play while I stretched my hurt leg. I'd just been raving to Trey and Indy, telling them how well they can scooter and skateboard, when out of nowhere a massive grasshopper jumped right next to me on the porch steps!

I have a healthy respect for big bugs. If I see a small spider, I can kill it. But if it's a tarantula—I'm not about to use a thin toilet paper barrier to feel it burst beneath my fingers.

So, the lord of all grasshoppers eyed me with his beautiful emerald eyes, turned to watch my children, and sat like a dog! He was so regal, so perfectly majestic sitting there, shining in all his glory like an expensive knickknack. And I became completely captivated.

I didn't move, not wanting this massive creature to leave my side. After about five minutes, my son jogged over, jolted up the stairs, and ran inside to get some water.

I let out a muffled cry because next to me twitched the beautiful, *slightly squashed*, bug! He'd lost a leg. After a moment, he tried standing, but simply turned in circles over and over on his side.

A woman must have heard me cry out because she ran over from the street. "Is everything okay? Are you all right?"

When I pointed to the spinner next to me, she broke out laughing. "You're kidding, right?"

"Is everything okay?" a man yelled from the street.

What the hell was happening? Was our entire town out for a jog—in front of my house?

"You never would've made it on a farm," she said. Then the woman turned away from me. "Hey, John. She's fine. Just too innocent for this world."

Anger welled up inside me. Someone had used those same words about Zeke, my angel baby, right before he died. "Too innocent." Who were they to judge me? At least I wasn't wearing a sports bra and wedgie shorts in public.

Indy came over and looked at the flailing grasshopper. "Wow, you really loved him, didn't you?" she whispered.

"He was just... so awesome. But now something is wrong with him."

Just like I knew *something* was wrong with me.

When Trey returned from the house, we tried to help the grasshopper stand, but he kept falling. "Oh, my gosh!" I quaked.

"We're giving him multiple concussions!" Trey said. "Mom, he's gonna die!"

An old truck rumbled into the driveway. Mike jumped out, so happy to be off work.

"What's wrong?" His smile flatlined after seeing my concern.

"This!"

"Um... it's a bug."

"But it isn't just any bug. He's broken now—like I know I am. You should've seen how kingly and majest—"

Mike kicked him into our flowerbed and then placed a rock on him. "And now he's out of his misery."

Mike and the kids went inside. Indy mouthed through the screen door, "I'm sorry, Mama." Empathy... it must be genetic.

And I stayed on the steps.

I innately knew a laborious, painful journey waited in my future. Only a few weeks later, a radiologist finally discovered the cancer.

It sounds so arbitrary to remember the king of all grasshoppers, but it just shows how the little things stand out when we're having a hard time.

Some people are dying to live healthy lives, while other people start livin' when they're dyin'.

CHAPTER 6
Lions and River Monsters

Mike and I split up in the store, and about ten minutes later I discovered they were literally out of everything we needed (stupid COVID-19 pandemic). My pace slowed, and I limped badly even with my walker.

A woman rushed into the aisle at that point, but when she saw me, she slowed and sauntered behind me on my trek down the world's longest aisle.

I turned a corner at the end of *our* long journey, and the woman darted in front of me.

"I feel so compelled to tell you," she said very loudly and slowly, "you're doing great."

As she walked away, tears filled my eyes, and I quietly cried for quite a while. Thank God no one really looks into people's eyes anymore, and no one noticed. My mask just got soaked—which was worse than meeting that woman.

Mike found me at that point. "What's wrong, sweetheart?"

"I just realized that I'm a charity case." I told him about the woman. "I know she meant well, but the way she said it, like I'm Frankenstein's monster or something. I mean, I know I just had radiation on my brain, but I can still understand English! And I'm just struggling to walk right now after surgery! I can do things. I'd like to have her come back here. There's gotta be something I can beat her at! Like Scrabble! Yeah. I could kick her ass at Scrabble!"

My husband—for some reason—seems perpetually amused by me. He hugged me in the store and chuckled. "Sure, you could beat her at something. And you know, she probably thought she was doing a really nice thing."

I just shook my head.

When we got home, I thought about my word for 2020: refinement. When I picked that word, I had no idea what the year would hold: cancer, humility, and a complete overhaul.

I know pride isn't always a terrible thing, but maybe it is when I can't recognize that people just want to be kind. After all, what the lady said was more for her benefit than for mine. And that's okay. Why should I fault her for wanting to feel gracious?

***

Several years ago, I made the executive decision to only say one negative thing a day.

This became even tougher after discovering I had cancer!

Throughout the hours, I'd catch myself getting ready to say something negative, but it wasn't quite bad enough to use my only negative comment of the day. Sometimes I've used it early—about eight a.m.— and then I have to be positive the rest of the day! Other times I'll forget to say something because I didn't find something quite bad enough.

Once, right after I started this, I chatted with a businesswoman who spoke quite negatively. Although she was working in a warm, cozy office—and drank a coffee — she talked about how terrible her job is and how much she hates the weather. No matter what I said, she flipped it negative.

It went on until I became almost mystified with how artfully she changed good to bad.

"Isn't it terrible here in Idaho? Don't you agree?" she finally asked.

"Ma'am, I only use one negative comment a day, and I'm not going to waste it on this."

Her faced paled a little before reddening. I really didn't mean to offend her, but I didn't want to waste my comment on that.

Anyway, I had to visit her office later. It was busy, and she didn't know I stood in the back of a line.

"I know you're upset," I heard her tell a customer, "but I only use one negative comment a day, and I'm not going to use it on this."

When it was my turn, she didn't act overly excited to see me, but I had to inwardly smile.

Even when you don't know you're making a difference, you just might be. Positivity wins out every time.

***

I heard from a friend today who has terminal cancer. He's had it for a year though, and now it's invaded his stomach, liver, and lungs. The tumor started in his spine which is all too real for me.

After I spoke with him, the pain in his voice stayed with me like a bad spirit. I just couldn't shake how much he reflects death right now. He said people get awkward when they talk to him lately; I think it's because people are so scared to die.

For some damn reason I ended up watching Animal Planet later. I saw a lion take down a gazelle — and it wasn't a quick death either. The thing was still alive and watching helplessly as the lion gnawed on it.

The whole time I was thinking, "That lion is cancer, and the gazelle is my friend. The gazelle is *me*. We just want to get away, but it's this slow, painful sort of ordeal where you just hope someone will save you from the jaws of the lion."

I turned off the TV. Nobody has time for that. I've always wanted to be a lion. Always. But right now, I'm praying for something to save me.

Being at the mercy of something puts things in perspective. Some things have never looked so clear.

***

This whole "facing death" thought had me doubting everything. I wondered if I'd been a good mother. It's tough raising four kids. My second oldest daughter even ran away to live with her biological father a week before my cancer diagnosis. That's been one of the hardest experiences of my life.

Earlier this summer, I'd wanted to bring the kids to float the Portneuf River, but it was so hard coordinating it with everyone. When we *finally* set the day, someone had the great idea that instead of getting six tubes, we should buy one giant tube to save money.

That was a mistake!

So, there we were, floating the Portneuf together, but it was extremely uncomfortable. And everyone (except Mike) kept complaining. Being a constant Pollyanna, I responded, "But it's a beautiful day."

"It's too hot."

"I'm uncomfortable."

"I want to go home."

"When will we be done? I have plans with my boyfriend later."

"Two to three hours," I said. "We get that much time to just enjoy each other. Won't that be amazing?"

But none of the kids thought so.

"Oh my gosh! Look!" I scooped something out of the water — the world's tiniest fish skeleton. "It's so small!" I showed the kids. This impressed my son, but I thought my youngest might jump ship — or throw up.

When we hit some rapids and the tube popped, things started to get bad. Mike tried to hold the hole in the tube, but it was pretty big.

"I'm getting out. I want you guys to enjoy this!" So, I got out of the tube (which is what Mike had wanted to do). I folded the tube so it wouldn't leak any more, and I started dragging them down the shallow river. As I walked, I willed the day to get better.

I started singing, hoping that would help. And just into the fifth word, I slipped and fell into a massive hole in the mucky river!

Kids still talk about the legend of the Portneuf River monster. Well, my kids saw it that day. After I'd resurfaced from the world's deepest river hole, a string of profanities left my mouth that would make a prison warden cringe. Mud and gunk clung to my face. Mascara dripped from my eyes.

"What in the *bleep*? I've been looking forward to this *bleeping* day for months. Yet does anyone else want to enjoy it? No! What in the *bleep* is going on with everyone. This bleepedity, bleepin' bleep!"

We all got out of the tube at some point after that and climbed from the river. I was the only one who got stung by a strange plant on the way out.

It was hard dragging the huge, popped tube behind us. The kids stayed close to Mike, and I walked alone—the river monster who tried not to cry.

My hair was still covered in muck, and I momentarily wondered if I had a baby fish skeleton somewhere in my hair. Sky, my daughter who ended up running away, told Mike, "We were having a great time until Mom flipped out."

And I felt terrible. Sometimes in life we can try so hard it becomes more stressful than it should be. But as I look back at my life, I worry my kids will remember more of these moments than not. The scary thing is it doesn't really matter anymore, the jobs I've had, the number of books I've written, the cool places I've played my violin. *Those* things don't matter. Was I a good mom and wife? Was I a good friend?

I've succeeded, and I've also really failed.

But the best thing about death is that it has a way of showing what's important. And like that failed trip down the Portneuf River, I don't want people— especially my children—to remember me like that river monster.

CHAPTER 7
Mornin' to Ya!

"Good mornin' to ya!" I practically hollered.

The elderly man turned, came well within six feet of me, and looked deep into my eyes. "I know this is hard on all of us," he said. "You hang in there! Good mornin' — to you!" I could almost see his huge grin despite that hospital mask.

I don't know why, but as he marched away, the gravity of the moment hit me. It's because this *is* hard on so many people. It's hard getting treatments and feeling sick from operations. It's hard trying to make things better for family and friends who are struggling with the news.

I just watched him and wished I could fix everyone in that damn cancer building.

But I can't.

So, I'd keep fiddling for strangers, making the waiting rooms "lively," and yelling "good mornin'" to anyone unlucky enough to cross my path.

This might be tough, but I vowed to be tougher.

Remember that saying, "God doesn't give us anything we can't handle"? I like what someone else added: "Well then, God thinks I'm a badass."

***

I got to see someone ring the bell. That means their cancer treatments are over. Instead of watching the woman who celebrated this big win, I watched the three patients who sat near me. Two of them perched expectantly, as if they can't wait for their turn. The third's head fell as she clapped, making it obvious that she thinks she'll never ring the bell. I studied her dimmed eyes and stretched skin.

The nurse came back shortly after. I tried to smile brightly but seeing that patient's sadness had deeply affected me.

"Are you okay?" the nurse asked.

"Just a blip of sadness. But the real question is, how are you? You're working on a holiday. And you look pretty busy."

She smiled down at me. "It's interesting, but not many people ask how I'm doing here. It's not a bad thing, they're just going through so much."

We talked for a while, and she seemed a bit lighter after we'd joked and smiled. She even brought some of the laughter to the woman who'd seemed so sad when the bell rang. I was most grateful for that.

Life can be terribly hard. The best I can do is fight with everything in me, trying to make life better for those around. Even if they aren't physically sick, they're going through their own struggles too.

I wished I could wrap my arms around the woman who got chemo. I'd love to tell her how beautiful and strong she is. But I need to have faith that she's on the road meant for her.

***

It just hit me how much my life has changed since I got cancer. I have several good hours of every day when I can be around people and do things. But for the rest of the day, I lie in bed and sleep. When you only have so many hours, well, it changes everything.

I don't have time to waste on menial things. I used to work and then work some more. If I wasn't working for the newspaper, I was working for myself.

Now, truly realizing that time is numbered for all of us, my views have completely changed.

Yesterday, I spent the day doing unusual things (for me). My preteen daughter, Indy, put fake nails on me, which involved a lot of glue. My son, Trey, taught me how to do a trick with his balisong trainer knife. Try *that* with fake nails! I also got to talk about art with my oldest daughter and watch her play video games. I didn't get to talk with my second oldest. She's still living with her bio-dad and not wanting to talk with me. The counselor said it might be the cancer; sometimes kids have a hard time handling things like this. I honestly don't know what it is, but it hurts.

Yesterday afternoon, when I was resting for the millionth time, I told my husband how fortunate I am to have him and our kids. I have no idea what the point — or the meaning — of life is, but it's strange what happens when we only have a small window of time each day.

I hate what cancer has done to me. It's still excruciatingly hard to walk, and I'm in a lot of pain, but I'm so grateful for the other changes it's caused in me. It's not all bad.

I'm grateful for time, even if it is only a window each day.

CHAPTER 8
The Hard Part

We've told the kids that I have cancer—when you're in this situation you have to. But we haven't told our two youngest that it might be terminal. After all, medical research progresses every day—and unless you're in an Orson Scott Card novel, it's hard to kill a Stilson (my maiden name).

But kids are like miniature detectives, and they catch much more than we realize. I remembered this last night.

I'd gone to sleep around six. One of the tumors is in my hip, and unfortunately it must be growing because when I lie on my right side a searing pain shoots up my body as if I'm getting tased where the tumor is. I'd been asleep for a few hours when a tiny knock resounded from my bedroom door.

"Yes?" I asked.

"Mama, it's Indy. Can I come in?"

Indy is quite small for her age, and awfully extraordinary. But as she walked in, she didn't light up the room like she normally does, and that worried me.

"I need to know," she said emphatically. "Are you dying?"

I blinked. "I'm really sick right now, sweetheart. But I'm fighting! And some of those doctors have no idea how tough I am."

"You missed story time tonight," she said. "You never miss it—not really. You must be so sick!" Then she climbed into bed with me and cried really hard. "I'm just scared, Mama. I can't even go to sleep without you reading to me. How am I supposed to *live* without you?"

I tried to keep my voice from quivering, but hearing her words hurt more than when I had the back surgery, radiation, or all of it combined. "I'm stronger than this," I told her. "I really am. But right now, we need to trust that God has a plan. Everything will be all right."

I hugged her for the longest time. Being in pain—I can handle. Most of the emotional stuff can be theorized into submission. But that—seeing my ten-year-old cry—that was a pain so terrible I could barely handle it.

I would do anything to protect her, and now my sickness is the source of her pain.

"Wait a minute. You're not crying just because I'm sick. You're crying about dinner."

"Huh?" She turned to me.

"You're bummed we didn't put mushrooms in it."

"Yuck!"

"And you wanted fish!"

She broke out laughing and wiped her tears away. "That sounds gross, Mama. I am not crying because I wanted mushrooms and fish!" She smiled.

She's such a blessing.

"I always wanted you," I said.

"And I always wanted you!"

Before she left the room, she kissed my cheek with those lips that are still so tiny. "Fine," she said. "If you can be strong, then so can I."

But after she left the room, I cried because I had missed story time and because I don't want to miss any number of things now *or* when the kids grow up.

I breathed slowly. "God has a plan," I told myself. "There's good buried in this, and God really does have a plan." With that in mind, I drifted back to sleep where I dreamed that I could walk normally and even run—and that I didn't have a care in the world.

***

It's been a weird day. I woke up to find quite a bit of tiny hairs resting on my pillow. In the mirror, another bald spot the size of Milwaukee stared back at me. Odd fact, it wasn't even on my radiation site. Oh joy.

Mike felt so bad he bought me some hair glue. It's not meant to glue in hair that has fallen out—thank God. It's used to help hide the bald spots. Unfortunately, it makes me look like an old man with comb-overs in very odd places. Fortunately, some friends have bought me scarves and hats.

The funny thing about balding—and I might need to ask some of the men from my graduating class—but maybe it makes people feel mortal.

I'm trying to be funny. Did you catch that?

Anyway, this brought up the topic of mortality again. It didn't help that a friend called to tell me about Christ right after more of my hair started falling out.

I've had many family members talk with me about Christianity—because I'm an idiot who recently announced *on social media* that I don't believe Jesus was the son of God.

To make a long story short, this disbelief happened nearly two decades ago when my little boy died. My faith in God grew, but my faith in Jesus diminished. Don't get me wrong, I *want* to believe in Jesus. I'm doing another Bible study now, hoping I'll believe again. I cherish the Old Testament, and I love God with all my heart, but I can't wrap my mind around Jesus.

I said this to my friend, and she told me I'm going to hell. She really believes that if I don't accept Jesus, I'm doomed.

After I finished talking with her, I went to lunch with a confidant who's in his late eighties and one of the most intellectual people I know. He always calls me "Mona," because he said people want to know why I smile.

As I told him that I'm apparently going to hell, he became so serious he didn't even use my nickname. He just looked at me with piercing blue eyes and said, "Don't worry about it. It's already figured out."

I can't explain why, but the idea of predestination is a bit comforting. It just makes me feel like I need to do the best I can and research. The rest will follow.

So, I might not have much hair — and I might not have much faith — but I'm trying.

***

My oldest daughter, Ruby, asked me out for lunch, and I could hardly wait for Sunday to roll around. Time seems so fleeting.

When the day finally came, we sat at the bar of the diner, and I did what I always do — I pulled out a deck of cards and dealt us both a hand.

She laughed and looked around. "People don't normally do stuff like this."

I just smiled. "I guess that's true, but it's my thing."

So, we played a few hands, laughed, and joked. It wasn't until our food came that things got serious. I started thinking about what has really given my life meaning. I looked at my gorgeous daughter — who shaved her head, losing all that beautiful hair to support me. She has stuck with me and been so kind these past months, growing up much faster than anyone should have to. Looking at *her*, I realized that the greatest thing I could ever do is make sure that the people who matter most know that I love them.

"Life has been hard," I said. "But you've been my little best friend through it all — since I was eighteen. So much of what got me through... was you." My kids are my heart.

She bit her lip, smiled, and started telling me something she'd obviously thought about for a while. Over our coffees, hash browns, and eggs, Ruby said how proud she is of the way I've lived my life and of how I've raised her.

Her love in that moment erased all the worry. I *knew* my life has had meaning. It wasn't because of what I've done for strangers, or if I've impacted people I barely know. I made a difference for someone who matters the most.

When you're facing death and things become clear, these are the affirmations you need to hear. At least for my beautiful Ruby, she'll carry good memories of me when my body gives out. Maybe those memories of playing cards in restaurants will carry on. But most of all, I hope she'll remember how much I love her with a resolve that can never be tamed, not even by death.

***

My sixteen-year-old daughter, Sky, ran away about a week before I found out I have cancer. She's living with her bio-dad now — and seems to be really happy — but the entire situation has left a hole in my heart that doesn't feel like it'll ever heal.

I guess I deserve it. I ran away from home when I was seventeen, became a homeless street musician, and lived on the beaches of Hawaii for a while.

I talked with my mom the other day, and it's a bit odd how we could relate on yet another level. My voice turned heavy with regret, and I told her how sorry I am for doing that to her. "I just didn't understand how much I hurt you. Not until now."

Last night I dreamed my daughter ran away again, but this time it was to come back to *my* house. I glowed, so happy to have her home, hold her in my arms, and tell her how much I've missed her.

When I woke up, she still wasn't here, but the cancer was. I sleep so much, and it's such a challenge to get around. And even months before I found out I had cancer, before she ran away, I only slept an hour each night because of the pain. I'm sure I wasn't fun and bouncy like I used to be. The cancer had changed me before we even knew it had taken hold.

So, today, instead of feeling strong, I feel pathetic, rejected, and weak. I know things will get better — they have to — but today is hard.

People keep telling me that teenagers are tough to raise, and the best thing we can do is show love. I love each of my children so much more than they know. I guess if I do die within the next two years, the kids will have some things left from me, like the books I've written. If they miss me, they can read those and remember. I just hope they'll know how very much I love them. The best thing I could leave behind isn't books though, or even money, or any of that. It's really just love.

I don't know what will happen tomorrow, but the doctor said I need to stop focusing on anything that could cause stress. Once again, I'm trying to remember that although He has much bigger things to worry about, God has a plan for me — and all of us.

I do think I'm being stripped of things for a reason: health, pride, even family. Once you get to the bare bones of a situation, then you can learn more about it. I'm learning an awful lot about myself, even through the pain.

CHAPTER 9
Baby Ruby

I'm twenty years old. My marriage is in shambles, and, as such, I'm the sole breadwinner, working two jobs just to pay the mortgage. But this isn't a sad day. I sit in a carpeted hallway, expectantly facing a closed white door. I have an entire day off—and adventure awaits!

It seems like forever and unfortunately my eyes keep wandering to another door that conceals a bedroom down the hallway. But I tell myself to never go down there. Ever.

I'm just about to get sucked down the hall, when I hear a little noise, something I've been waiting for.

I open the white door and can hardly contain my joy. My very own princess, my perfect baby stands in her crib. Curly hair frames her face, and she giggles when she sees me. We are heaven—to each other. I whisk her up, and we spin.

The morning is a blur of reading, singing, and playing. I hold her on my hip and cook up new ideas for lunch. But I only finish when she's tasted the final product, and she points her chubby finger in approval.

After she eats, I clean her up, and her long eyelashes start to flutter. But I don't just want to put her in bed. She falls asleep, finally closing her eyes after staring into mine with such love. And I hold her there in my arms. I don't care how we're both so young, or how tired I am from working too many hours, or how worried I am about divorce. My baby, well, she's *my* world.

After a while, I bring Ruby to her crib and cover her with the best blanket we own.

It's only then that I can't resist the pull down the hallway. There's another crib in there, an empty crib. Tears flood my eyes as I remember my first baby boy. And I must have been there a long time. After an eternity of silence, I hear my little girl down the hallway.

I rush to her, whisk her up again and hold her tight. She hugs me back, always making everything better. I wipe my eyes so she won't know anything's wrong, kiss her on the forehead, and ask what adventure we should go on next. We pull out her blocks, and instead of focusing on things that are broken and sad, the two of us begin building.

This memory returned this week when I threw up blood. Turns out I needed to come off my blood thinner for a little while even though I've had two blood clots in my lungs in the past.

I remembered those times with Ruby—and all the great moments I've had with my kids. I told myself that despite pain and the fear it inevitably brings, my family and friends keep me strong.

In life, we often have two doors to choose from. Regardless of our circumstances, instead of regret and bitterness, choose love.

CHAPTER 10
Fear

I started this arbitrary thing years ago. Whenever I'd even begin to get agitated over something stupid, I would stop myself and think, "What if I were dead? What *if* God let me come back for this one single day? Would I have time to be agitated, hurt, or annoyed about much of anything?" Maybe not!

Yesterday, as I tried going to sleep, my back pulsed from the surgery where they removed my tumorous vertebrae, the nausea was overpowering, and I had a new headache from last month's radiation. I kept thinking how my two youngest are seeing counselors to deal with the fact that I have cancer — and how this makes me feel terrible they're going through this too. It's heart-wrenching to answer some of their questions about death.

My brain automatically went to the old thought that used to catapult me into gratitude: "What if I were dead? What if God let me come back for this one single day?"

But death was too close right now, and gratefulness eluded me. Instead, I thought about those things that have always plagued humanity. What if I'm on the road to death right now? Yes, we all are, but I mean, maybe this is too fast. The Japanese bullet train to death. Irrevocably sick in my thirties.

Like several doctors had said, I might only have two years to live—which means I'll just get sicker and sicker, watching myself and my loved ones suffer, then I'll die.

Or maybe I'll beat this. I've had dozens of people tell me that if anyone can overcome this, it's me.

But instead of this making me feel better, I felt fear.

My husband came into the room. He's usually really loud and silly, but he knows how to be quiet and gentle too. He encircled me in his strong arms and just let me cry.

I knew I had to shake myself of this self-pity quickly. So, as I cried, I started listing what I'm grateful for. "I'm glad I'm still alive. I'm grateful I even have people to worry about—people who would miss me if I'm gone. I'm grateful for snow and a beautiful view where I can see deer...."

The list went on.

And soon, I stopped crying.

I fell asleep like that. And even though things could be better, I also realize they could be much worse.

***

Sky came home for the weekend. We were all surprised, but I wasn't about to ask questions. I just wanted to make this fun and exciting so hopefully she'll want to move back home. So, we brought all the kids out to eat. I used my walker, which is always a bit embarrassing, but when we got to the table my husband hid the contraption and after the waiter brought us our waters, I got an idea. Life is too hard right now; we needed to make a fun memory while all of us were together.

"Everybody, I want to make a bet!" I said.

My husband's eyes filled with mirth as if to say, "Here we go again."

"I will bet you twenty-one dollars, that you can't guess the waiter's age."

They were all interested now, everyone except my son, Trey. "That might not be very nice."

"He seems like a good sport," I said.

"Yeah," interjected Ruby, "he's not gonna care. But how will we do this?"

"Each of you pick an age, and I'll write it down. Whoever is the closest will win the money."

"Whoever is the closest without busting," Mike said.

I nodded. "Agreed. Whoever is the closest without busting. Sky, what's your guess?"

I quietly gathered each guess, and when *anyone* walked by, we went silent. Except at one point when we were laughing so hard that I almost spit out my water!

The waiter finally showed up and asked what we'd like.

"We kind of have a bet going," my husband said.

"Yeah," I followed up, "we're teaching our kids how to gamble. Because we're those parents."

The waiter burst out laughing, and then Mike asked him for his age.

"Well, I'll tell you my age, but what do I get out of it?"

"A really good tip!" I piped in.

"Well, okay." He looked around. "I'm forty."

Our youngest daughter nearly shot from her seat. "Me! It was me! I guessed forty."

"Wait," the waiter said. "What did everyone else guess?"

"The youngest guess was thirty-five," I said.

"And some were over forty?" The heavily tattooed waiter smirked as he teased us. "Gee thanks, guys."

We ate our food and had the most wonderful time. When the waiter came back for the last time, he said, "I'm stuck here working all day. I wish I could go home with you guys."

Mike laughed. "That's not the first time we've heard that from a waiter."

"It's actually not." I laughed so hard because we always bring a deck of cards or have something silly up our sleeves.

We left an amazing tip, and our kindhearted little boy even left his allowance—saying he couldn't wait for the guy to get it "because he'd been so nice to us."

As I saw each of my kids' smiling faces, I had to reflect. For a minute, I forgot about the pain and the cancer. Despite my hunched back and lack of hair, I was really living—like I used to years before this diagnosis. And it hit me, whether people have a bad diagnosis—or just a bad outlook—we should all choose to make the best of the moments we have and just live. Finding the good and sharing it with others, that's what makes life really *worth* living.

Sky decided to go back to her dad's the next day. I miss her so much it hurts, but I'm still just trying to be thankful that she came home to see us at all. I think she's shocked with how sick I am. That must've been strange seeing how different things are since I got diagnosed with cancer. I think seeing me like this is harder than she wants to admit. I wonder if it's one of the things keeping her away.

***

I entered the funeral home, and the director greeted me as if he knew I didn't belong there. His graying hand shook my energetic one, and our eyes met. Two more opposite people had never stood so close before. He motioned — at the speed of molasses — silently denoting the morbid conveyor belt of people who waited to see the corpse of my high school friend.

His young bride cried so loud that people in other states heard her. And who could blame her; he was a great guy. In fact, we hadn't talked since junior year. I was his wing-woman as we dragged Main in a souped-up Mustang. Years before. Yet here I stood, behind this army of people, wanting to say goodbye in case his spirit haunted the room.

After infinity, it was my turn, and I childishly peeked into the casket. There he rested at twenty-seven. He'd never smoked, but lung cancer didn't care. I whispered, "You were one of the good ones."

His wife looked at me oddly.

"High school friend," I said. "I was like one of the dudes." And I realized she wasn't a person who said 'dudes' or spoke to people who did. "Well, sorry for your loss."

I didn't belong there, and I knew it. So, I walked back to the door. I wondered what brought everyone else to see his body: love, respect, curiosity, a chance to face their own mortality?

A man stopped me on the way out. "Makes you appreciate every moment."

"Sure does," I said. And I wondered if he knew my friend or if he was one of those funeral crashers who goes to remember that he has so much to be grateful for — since he's not dead yet.

I remembered all of this today as I daydreamed, but as I got to the casket, instead of my friend, I saw *myself* there — all plastic and stiff-faced, stuck in that stuffy box, hands crossed oddly, face painted with bright makeup that I'd never really wear.

I tried to shake these thoughts, but they overpowered me — so terrifying I could hardly breathe. It was a real panic attack, that's for sure.

Mike held me when he saw me folding under the pressure. "It's okay. It's okay."

His touch is so magical that I swear he could tame a wild animal — that's why I married him. My heart finally slowed back down, and he read a couple chapters of a book to me; it's a book about gratitude.

I know I need to be positive, but today was hard. The doc said the treatments still need more time to shrink things. It's just a waiting game.

So, I need to distract myself and do something nice for someone else. I might go play my violin at a nursing home tomorrow. I'll have to sit. I won't be able to play long, but at least I'll get to do something that always heals my mind no matter how scared I get.

I don't want to dwell on the past or worry about the future when I should be appreciating every second I have.

My poor friend. I still wonder what he thinks of heaven.

CHAPTER 11
Animals and Grief

For several years we've had two cats, one black and one white. They couldn't be more opposite. One likes people and the other one just likes *one* person. They fight all the time, and when the black one isn't sneaking onto the counter to find food, the white one is just trying to find some peace and quiet.

When I first got sick with cancer, the black cat started stalking me. Every time I'd sit down, he'd practically mirror my presence. I'd sit; he'd sit. I'd walk; he'd walk. It seemed like he knew how bad I felt—and he wanted to make me better. Meanwhile, the white cat just stared at us like we were crazy. His eyes turned to judgmental slits as he licked his regal paws.

On Monday, our black cat, Cole, didn't seem quite right. He flopped onto my lap, nuzzling lethargically up to me. On Tuesday, when Mike took him to the vet, Cole died. It's hard thinking he's no longer around to follow me and check up on me, even when I didn't want him to. I realized how much I enjoyed checking up on him, too.

Yesterday morning was so lonely, I thought I'd snuggle the white cat—the king—but I changed my mind before even trying. He doesn't like anyone except Sky, who he was missing terribly since left to live with her dad. All day, he sits away from people and just wants his fancy food and his space.

My son said, "It's just so weird that he's gone. And he can't come back."

The conversation turned to my cancer and how several doctors have only given me a certain amount of time to live. I want to have hope that I can get better, but I also don't want to hide from facts either. I know death is final, a sobering reality to a sometimes even more sobering world, but if that's what God wants, well, my life has always been in His hands. And my kids deserve to hear the truth.

Still, seeing my son's widening eyes, hearing that he finally understood the irrevocable truth about death and that he knew what we might be facing as a family, that weighed heavily on my heart.

I cried for the lost moments, and for the future ones I might miss. I cried because I want to protect my kids from the pains of the world, but right now my sickness is a source of that very pain. The sadness was so deep, so strong, my chest and insides ached from the heaviness of it all.

And as I cried, out of nowhere, the white cat sauntered around the corner, jumped on my stomach, and stared at me!

We both held each other's gaze for a while. He's never sat on me before, and I didn't quite know what to do. Then he snuggled down, stretched his paw over my shoulder, and simply fell asleep.

I looked around, bewildered as the cat purred. There wasn't time to cry anymore. Now I was in shock. How had he known I needed something exactly like this?

I don't know why, but I felt so much healing emanate from the exact cat who used to hate me.

I closed my eyes, and we both slept—me in the somberness of the moment, and my kingly cat who'd stepped down from his throne to make sure I was okay.

Death can be hard, but it really does offer the perspective of gratitude for those brave enough to embrace change.

***

We waited a week to bury our cat. Honestly, I was a little creeped out. We stored his body in our cold garage, and I kept seeing something black out of the corner of my eye. Maybe I just want him to be alive.

Anyway, it finally came time for us to have the funeral with the kids there. They appeared ready to dig the hole, send good wishes, and say goodbye. It took a long time for me to walk to the back corner of our yard. My legs still don't work right and my back hunches over awkwardly. But Mike helped me lumber down there, and as we stood at Cole's resting place, I found the location fitting.

It's strange, but we've had unusual experiences in that corner of the yard. Once a deer died there, and the neighbors called to tell us something was rotting behind our shed. Fish and Game came to take it away. By the time they arrived, the smell was nauseating.

Years later we found another deer there—in the exact same spot! It was injured and not strong enough to jump the fence. We named her Debbie and started giving her little treats to sustain her. She slept by the kids' basement windows, huddling next to the warmth of the house. And soon enough, Debbie got her strength back and, without a goodbye, she left. I guess life can be like that sometimes. We can help others, but that doesn't mean they'll be in our lives forever. I just felt bad I never got to say goodbye.

So that's where we buried Cole, where we found both a dead and a living deer. I somehow wished we could bring Cole back, but books have told me *that's* a bad idea. I'd much rather Cole stay dead than turn into a murderous zombie.

I'm glad the kids got to say goodbye, and that we no longer have a dead animal in our garage—even if I did love him when he was alive.

Death can be so hard, but having a chance to say goodbye somehow makes it a little easier.

As we held Cole's funeral, I wondered about my own. The kids each said who Cole had been to them.

What have I been to them or to anyone really? Do the memories of what remains about us somehow embody who we truly are? I wonder....

CHAPTER 12
Creeps and Anchors

I hadn't been driving much because the pain from the tumors had gotten notably worse, and I struggled with stamina. But I needed to get out and see strangers and a store filled with modern conveniences that people take for granted — like peanut butter.

I used a grocery cart instead of my walker and had only grabbed a few light items when my hip and leg started throbbing. I limped to the front of the store. I'd need to sit down after I paid, or call Mike to come and pick me up.

I smiled at the cashier who was still helping someone else. She didn't need to know I was in pain and that I kept having dreams about a long, cancerous death.

The guy in front of me seemed like a total jerk. You know the kind. He still wore his class ring two decades after graduation. He had bling all over the butt of his jeans. His shirt was a size too small to show off his huge muscles. *See how good I am at not judging?*

He flirted with the young cashier and then started ranting. "This was the worst year of my life. The day sports got canceled was the worst day ever. And now we have to wear masks! I can't even see what you really look like," he told the cashier.

As he continued complaining, I had to stop myself from ripping him apart. I'm normally so sweet and nice—a doormat when I should take a stand. Yet, this man enraged me.

He thought he had it bad? Because he *can't* work out? And he *can't* bring girls to his favorite restaurant. And he has to wear a mask!

I made up the whole monologue in my head as I slumped over the cart, my right leg shaking because I needed to sit down. I wanted to say, "Try having cancer. Try being told you will die within two years. Try explaining death to a couple of teenagers and two preteens. While you're busy worrying about sports and women, I'm fighting for my life, losing my hair and my dignity, scared shitless that I'll die before my baby is eighteen and my kids' lives will be turned upside down. So, before you go on about how shitty your life is, think about the lives lost because of COVID, the people separated from their families as they died. Hell, even think of me contemplating funeral arrangements before I'm even forty years old."

Before I could say any of this, he took his bags and left.

"What a creep," the cashier whispered. "He could have kids my age."

I sat on a bench at the front of the store. Then I thought about how I shouldn't judge. I guess those things are hard for him; he doesn't know any better. But it would be so nice if people like that could break free from their bubbles and realize how lucky they really are. He's healthy. Instead of complaining—he should just go live!

***

Years ago, I worked as a receptionist. I'll never forget the day when my coworker confessed something. "I have terminal cancer," she'd said. The woman hadn't done the greatest job at work up until that point, and I'd wondered how she still had her job. "I put in my notice because I can't work much longer. But I wanted you to know. You've always been so nice to me."

"Why didn't you tell me before?" I asked, feeling badly for judging her previously.

"Well, when people know I'm sick, they treat me differently—like there's something wrong with me. And I guess there is, but you know, I don't want to be treated that way. And then usually that's all they want to talk about."

"You're really dying?" I couldn't stop myself.

"Yeah, but I'm at peace with it. My youngest is a junior, but at least I've been with him this long."

The cavalier way she talked about death shocked me. My impulse was to tell her to have faith, that she would absolutely recover. But I stopped myself. I suddenly understood her nearly translucent skin that hung loose, her tired eyes. I realized her hair must have been a wig for all those months.

"Can I take you out for dinner and drinks? Since you put in your notice, and I wanna wish you well."

"Um, sure! All right! I can't drink alcohol, but I would love to go out."

We met with one of the other receptionists at a local restaurant. I ordered a little too much to drink as I thought about this poor woman's fate. But I didn't say any of that to her. Instead, we had the best time laughing and joking. At one point we laughed so hard I almost spewed my drink and had to use a napkin to wipe my chin. But none of us said a word about cancer or death.

On her last day at work, she gave me an anchor necklace—always thinking about other people instead of herself. "This is what you've been to me," she said. "You made me laugh—every single day. And you treated me like nothing was wrong. You've been my anchor."

"But I didn't know anything was wrong."

"You knew at the restaurant."

She gave me such a tight hug. She'd become so tiny and frail. Tears flooded my eyes as reality hit.

Over the following weeks and months, we'd talk and text, but it still came as a shock when I read her obituary. That day I donned my anchor necklace, proudly wore it to work, and thought of a woman who had changed my life.

It's surreal now that I have cancer. I think of my friend so often. How strange that even after she's gone, now she's somehow become an anchor for me.

***

As I drove through the snow-infested mountains from Utah to Idaho, with the wind nearly ripping our truck from the road, I thought about Zeke, my son who died on January 30, 2003. I shook my head, telling myself to remain calm. This drive was dangerous enough, without me turning into an emotional basket case.

I didn't recall all of the sad circumstances of his death. Instead, I simply remembered a specific day, nearly a month before he died.

Zeke's nurse had said I could hold him in a rocking chair. Right before she was about to pass him to me, he started crying really hard. Another nurse came by and said I shouldn't hold him, that they needed to up his vent settings. But I pleaded, *begging* them to let me hold my baby. They reluctantly handed him to me.

I rocked slowly, careful since he had so much tubing in him. Instead of crying harder like they'd thought he might, he melted into my arms, always meant to be there. I put my pinkie near his hand, and he wrapped his little fingers around it, holding on so damn tight. Tears filled my eyes as I rocked him forever. In that moment, it didn't matter how sick he was or how hard this was. We loved each other. Nothing could take that away, not time, not sickness, not death. And that moment, amid the stench of medicine and all those whirring machines, that was a perfect moment.

I could hardly believe how many years it's been as I blinked, focusing on the road ahead. The weather began clearing a little, and it wasn't quite so terrifying.

After we were safely home and all the kids were in bed, I told Mike about the memory. "I can't really remember the bad parts of Zeke's life anymore, but I remember every detail of holding him in the rocking chair for the first time."

Mike squeezed my hand.

"It's crazy, Mike, but I feel so much peace right now. When time has passed and everything else is gone, all that remains — all that really matters — is love."

And so now when I think of Zeke, the memory of his love is in the forefront of my mind. I hope that's what he remembers about me as well.

CHAPTER 13
White Feathers and Hope

My mom used to tell me that if I found a white feather it meant an angel was around, looking out for me. I didn't believe her, even if it was a neat idea. As the days have passed, I've sure wished an angel could be here, with me as I fight cancer.

My oldest daughter paid for me to have a wig fitting. The two beauticians pulled a stocking over my scalp, and Mike helped me pick wigs we both thought would be cute. We all laughed and joked about a white bob.

I said, "Well, I'm glad I finally found something worse than cancer. It's *that* wig!"

About halfway through the session, as if the music slowed to more foreboding melodies, I looked in the mirror, and the gravity of the situation hit me.

I looked so much different than six months ago. How much worse might I look within the next year? The magnitude of stage four cancer falls on me in waves every once in a while. I never know when or where the sadness will hit. I wished again that someone somewhere—even if it were an angel—could be looking out for me right now. But even if God is as real as ever, angels have begun to feel like the Tooth Fairy or the Easter Bunny, and as I continued looking in the mirror, I rushed to wipe away the tears before the beauticians or Mike could see.

I finally picked a wig, and the beauticians let me wear it home. The thing is a blond number, hanging just to my shoulders. It is meant to make me feel fun and free, but as we pulled into our driveway, I felt like an impostor.

The tears really came then. "What's wrong?" Mike asked gently, parking the car. "What do you need? Are you nauseous again?"

"No. Today, I'm just scared." It was a huge confession, something hard to even say out loud.

We stayed there, parked in the driveway. And as he held me, I gazed out the windshield.

Then, as if time had stopped, the strangest thing happened. When my fear was at the worst it's ever been, a white shape floated from the sky. I watched as it ebbed and flowed, barely swayed by the wind. The white feather landed on the windshield, resting *right* in front of me!

I immediately stopped crying. "Hang on," I told Mike and hobbled out of the car.

The feather remained despite gusts of wind. So, I gingerly picked it up, almost cradling the thing, and brought it back into the car.

"My mom always says that when you find a white feather like this, it means an angel is watching out for you." My voice caught on the words.

And as odd as it sounds, a realization folded through me, from the top of my head, down, through the rest of my being. A renewal so thick that it has stayed.

After we'd walked into the house, I hung up my wig, stared into the mirror and touched my own sheared hair. As I placed the white feather in my keepsake box, I shook my head.

Maybe even when things are at their worst, when we feel like they won't get better, someone, somewhere is looking out for us.

CHAPTER 14
The Kindest Eyes

A few Sundays ago, the Baptist pastor surprised me, calling me out by name during a prayer. And it wasn't short either. He prayed for my health, my renewed strength, but most of all, he prayed for God's will. This was all a shock because I'm not a member of that church; I still don't even believe in Jesus. I just like hearing the sermons. Yet, there they were, praying— for me.

After the service ended, a couple to our left gazed curiously, probably wondering why I hobbled or why I'd lost my hair. Now that the pastor had prayed for me, well, that incited even more interest.

Sometimes these humanly curious stares can make me uncomfortable, but they didn't that day. Instead, I met the older couple's eyes and smiled.

Time stopped.

It was an intimate moment shared between strangers. I wondered about it all week until Wednesday night when my son came home from youth group.

"Remember that man to the left of us in church? He was a little older?"

Of course I remembered the man with the kind eyes. "Yeah?"

"He died this week in an accident."

I had to sit down. It felt so surreal. To think, they'd been praying for me in church, when we should have been praying for him.

I might have been given an expiration date by the doctors, but this unexpected death was a stark reminder that all of us face the same inevitable end.

I wish I would've gotten that man's name. I looked over at my son. "It's so hard to believe he died. He really did have the kindest eyes."

***

Years ago, I visited an elementary school to cover a special news story for the newspaper. Everyone had already gone to an assembly, so no one could let me into the building. That day had been quite snowy, and the school's windows were a bit dirty from the morning's storm.

I knocked, but no one heard me. I tried all the doors; they remained locked. Then people flooded the hallways. I knocked again, waved, even yelled, but *no one* saw me.

Some of the teachers and kids appeared to look at me, but they couldn't see through the window. After a while, I just stood, shivering in the cold.

As I watched people laughing and smiling, I felt a little bit reflective, thinking of the irony. Sometimes I've felt like this in life, as if I'm knocking on a window where no one understands me or my true worth. I'd be capable of so much if just given the chance to "come in." Gifts and potential, waiting dormant, hoping anyone will answer the door. As I stood there, I wondered, "Is this what it feels like to be dead? Just watching people who can't see." Is that what I had felt for years?

Suddenly, a little boy and his teacher—from way down the hallway, behind everyone—spotted me. He waved and tugged on her sleeve. They both smiled wide and bolted down the hall to the door.

"You must be freezing! We've been waiting for you. They'll be so excited to talk with you and to be in the newspaper."

"How did you see me?" I asked. "No one else could."

"We've been waiting for you!" the little boy replied. "You're with the paper. It's a big deal!"

I walked in, and some snow fell from my hood. The teacher patted me on the back and, as the little boy went toward the auditorium, she said, "You're making such an impact in this area. We appreciate you and your positivity."

I bit my lip and as I walked into the auditorium, everything seemed brighter, better, such a contrast to the cold, dreary world I'd been freezing in moments before.

The kids squealed the moment I entered the room because they'd met me before, and I represented something they thought was awesome—a chance for their faces and stories to appear in a paper that had stayed in business for over one hundred years.

As I took picture after picture and answered questions for kids who love to write, I realized I should never feel like I'm locked outside, looking in on everyone else and wishing I had a purpose. After all, everyone has a purpose, even me. For a time, that was running a tiny newspaper and writing stories for the people of Bingham County. Now, it's finding the best in life even as I fight to survive cancer.

***

I limped back from the mailbox, so proud that I didn't need to use my walker. "Of course, the letter didn't come," I told myself. She died in 2020 and no matter how many trips I'd make to the mailbox, the letter wouldn't magically appear.

Fran was unlike anyone I've ever met, so energetic and full of sass. I loved joking around with her and seeing how she could make literally anything funny. It sounds trivial, but I looked forward to the birthday card she sent me each year because it meant she was still doing well, happy, and loved by everyone she met.

But this year I would never be able to talk with Fran again, and the hilarious birthday card wouldn't come. So, I told myself to stop checking the mailbox.

My birthday progressed — one of the best I've ever had. Despite pains from cancer and intermittent nausea, I really lived in the moment, enjoying my family with every bit of me. As I started opening my gifts, Indy, my youngest daughter, suddenly panicked. "The green envelope. Where is it? The green envelope. Have you seen it?"

I shook my head. "No. I haven't."

No one knew where it was.

"But I made you something really awesome! I have to find it." Then she got up and started rummaging through drawers that rest to the side of our kitchen. "Like this!" she spouted, before running over waving an envelope. "The envelope looks just like this one. Have you seen it?" She placed it on the table in front of me, and my eyes grew wide.

"Indy, where did you get this?"

"The last drawer, why?"

I held my breath as I picked up the envelope. It was unopened, postmarked December 13, 2018, addressed from Fran and her husband—back when they were both alive.

My hands shook as I opened the card. It felt as if Fran sat there with me, almost smirking because she'd somehow rigged the system. And when I pulled the card from the envelope, I burst out laughing. She'd sent me a holiday card with a duck on it. Of course, she had! Fran absolutely loved ducks so much that some people called her Fishducky.

I immediately told my family why this was such a strange thing. "It's from 2018! We always open our mail. And it was in the drawer with our tax returns. This is unreal."

That night, I clutched the card and thought of my dear friend. I looked up toward heaven.

"Oh, Fran, I sure hope you know how much I love you and how much your friendship has meant to me."

"Fran sounds like she was a character," someone said after I told them the story.

"Oh, she really was. She could make anything better. Even a birthday when she's no longer here."

***

Why do terrible things happen to good people? This is something I've been asked a lot—especially when someone finds out that I have cancer. But it hits me funny because I've always seen God as a clockmaker.

In my imagination, He works and works to build these intricate, multifaceted clocks and watches. They run for however long they're supposed to. Maybe a clock is caught in a house fire or an earthquake. A watch could be left out in the rain, even when it's not weatherproof. The clock might get cracked or worn with time. Maybe the thing lasts and lasts much longer than expected. But the point is that at some point, the clock will stop. When it's run its course, only a fool would blame the clockmaker. Cancer is terrible, but I'm not about to blame God. He gave me life — He wound my clock — death was just part of the bargain.

Our world is filled with so many terrible variables. But if something bad happens, it can usually look good with a change of perspective. Even a crack in a clock's face can look like a rainbow when turned in the right light. So, that's what I'm looking for today: rainbows. Sometimes even the biggest imperfections can make life beautiful.

CHAPTER 15
Biker in Heaven

I'm hiking, but I'm not alone. The man to my left appears to have stepped out of a biker bar. He's massive, muscles bulging from his sleeveless leather jacket. The whole thing makes me smile; I never imagined God to have a long, gray beard—or to look like such a legend.

We traverse rocky terrain and dangerous boulders. Even when I'm not looking directly at the man, I know He's there. Sometimes I'll catch His scent or hear His voice. Each time I almost fall, something helps me safely stay the course.

Finally, we reach the top of the mountain, but it's not what I expect, and my heart sinks. "God," I turn, "why are we here?"

His face wrinkles with sorrow, and as He stares at a stone altar, He doesn't say a word.

"What is this place?" I press on.

"This is where all men must be tested. The tests come at different times and in diverse ways, but they always come." He motions for me to hold out my hands. "Do you trust me?"

I nod and do what He asks despite my human desire to run.

God, that gnarly-looking biker, gently ties my hands before motioning for me to lie on the cold, stone slab.

"Am I going to die?" I ask.

"Everything has a season," He says.

My stomach turns. I'm so scared. But as I stare up into His eyes, I see the mysteries of the universe and understand that He knows so much more than I ever could. He must have a reason for all of this.

"I don't want to die," I say, my voice shaky as I sit on the stone altar. Then, ever so slowly, I swing my legs up and lie on my back.

"Close your eyes," He says.

And as I study His features for the last time, I realize this is what it must be like to fully surrender. "I... trust you," I whisper. And I believe wholeheartedly that whatever comes next is for the greater good.

***

I had several tests and scans yesterday. I'll have more tomorrow. But as I waited for results, I remembered the previous story and how it came to me long after reading the story of Abraham and Isaac in Genesis 22.

I have no idea what the future will hold, but I'm amazed how liberating it feels to finally let go. I have no control over this situation. It really is in God's hands now. I love how I picture Him. I bet He owns a Harley to ride on those streets of gold.

***

I've met a lot of people through this experience, but the new friend I think about often is a cantankerous woman who lives by me. She has terminal lymphoma, and she is not happy about it.

"It's such a beautiful day," I told her last week on the phone.

"If you like that sort of thing."

"It's just gorgeous. The sun is shining. The birds are singing."

"There you are, talking about the day when we both know we're dying."

"Everyone is dying," I say.

"But we're dying faster, and it's a slow, painful death. I hate my life. What did I do to deserve this?"

"I don't think either of us did something wrong. But while I'm going through this, I'm appreciating every day I can."

The conversation continued much the same until I told her how I'd be getting test results this week, and how I *might* get good news.

"But you might get terrible news," she practically spat the words.

I paused. I understood how this experience had beaten her down, but I didn't get why our responses were so different. I hung up the phone and kept wishing I could make her life better, easier. Just like she couldn't sober me the way she wanted to, I couldn't help her grasp onto hope. We're both stuck in the same situation — on opposite sides of a chasm — and no matter how much each of us wanted to help the other, we just couldn't.

I've met a lot of new people through sharing my story. People who live far away and close to home. There's a little boy heroically battling cancer; I read his updates and find strength in my own circumstances. There's an older lady who offers me sage advice and encouragement despite her own terminal situation. (All she thinks about is others.) Then there's a loving son who messages me and talks about the struggles his mother goes through as she fights for her life—all while finding the kindness to pray for me.

Cancer has been debilitating, to say the least, but because of this situation I've met so many people who have changed my life for the best. I don't have an answer for why this is happening to all of them, but for myself, I'm grateful for the lessons.

***

Today has been a sobering reality that I'm on a long, hard road. The doctor confirmed—again—that this probably is what I'll die from, but we just don't know when.

So, let's look at the positives:

No. 1 – I might have longer than two years.

No. 2 – Everything looks remarkably unchanged. They said, "Stability is not something to sneeze at." There is something exciting though! After radiation, my cancerous brain tumor is a little smaller than last time. What? That's awesome!

No. 3 – There's a support group for juveniles and young adults with cancer who are thirty-nine and under. I might have squeaked in at thirty-eight, but I'm still considered a young adult with cancer. Nothing like a cancer support group to make me feel young.

PS – I walked past a man with cancer who's probably forty—too bad that schmuck missed the cutoff (bwa-ha-ha).

So, the news isn't bad, and it isn't stellar. I'm a little deflated because it would've been super cool to be automatically cured like those folks in the Bible. But no. Apparently, I'm still terminal, I still have cancer, and I still have a brain tumor. Yep. That is hard to write.

Today, all of this is so hard to believe... again. I have days like that, you know, when reality is tough to digest.

Sincerely,

A Young Adult with Cancer

CHAPTER 16
Merely a Flesh Wound

There was a girl from high school, one of the cutest girls in town, but because she "walked funny," none of the guys asked her out. I thought about that girl a couple of months ago as I dressed in my hospital gown, then spotted my hunched, scarred body in the mirror. I hope Mike means it when he says he thinks I'm beautiful and that he's not embarrassed by how I look and move.

I turned from my reflection before hobbling to the next room where I'd wait to be called back for radiation. A woman slumped into a hospital chair beside me, later explaining she felt dejected because of a tumor in her head. Her treatments had caused a bumpy, purple rash to spread all around her right eye and cheek.

I offered a quiet greeting, acting like nothing was wrong, and before I knew it, the woman told me everything. She was mortified about the rash; people stared, but when she told them it was melanoma, no one thought it was a big deal. "They all say they've had skin cancer. But it's *not* what I have. And it's like they have no concept of what melanoma can do. I don't want them to minimize this."

We were quiet for a while. "I have melanoma, too," I admitted, and she was taken aback. "Stage four.

They had to remove my L3 vertebrae because a tumor had eaten the whole thing. That's why I can't stand up straight anymore." Another long pause. "You're right though. People don't understand how serious melanoma is. Other than that small aspect, I can't imagine what you're going through. I'm so sorry."

"Well, I don't have stage four. But there is something really tough about having it all over my face. It's really hard."

I never forgot the woman, so devastated and sad.

Time has passed, and I've thought about her often. But this week, I saw her again. I'd just gotten my IV, and was ready for my infusion and more scans, when I spotted her. She hobbled past, and I almost said hi when I realized she was missing an eye!

Sure, they patched the thing, but she'd recently had surgery to remove it because the melanoma had spread. I heard her mumble to the receptionist about what had happened, and I almost fell apart.

"I have to use the bathroom," I told my husband, and I hurried in there to cry. That woman—the sweet, scared woman—had been worried about a rash. How in *the hell* is she supposed to live without an eye? The whole thing hurt too much. I had to quell the pain rising in my chest because some of the things I've seen and heard since starting this journey, well, they're devastating.

After returning to my seat, I overheard a receptionist complaining about her boss and her job. It took everything in me not to walk up to that counter and smack her. Why? Because she still has both of her eyes!

A couple of times during my treatment Mike would catch me crying. "Are you okay?" he'd ask.

"Yeah, there's just so much to this that I never expected. I know these doctors are helping us, but it can also be torturous too. They took that woman's eye. I mean, I'm sure it saved her life, but.... It's just so hard seeing other people suffer."

I hate the whole concept that we should feel better about our own situation because someone else has it worse. Shouldn't that devastate us even more because we feel bad for ourselves and the other person? Yet, I caught myself thinking that way today. I'm grateful my tumors are all up my spine and my brain and not eating at my eyes. That poor woman.

She had a significant impact on my life, and she doesn't even know it. We met only briefly, and yet I'll pray for her every day. I hope she'll find the strength she needs to get through this. I can't imagine how hard it must be. And for her to have a stage of cancer that wasn't as bad as mine, yet now, she's facing something so much worse. Life can be so unpredictable.

***

I hate giving family and friends medical updates. If there's one thing I've learned about cancer, it's a roller coaster. And no one wants to hear the tedious difficulties of how it's better and then it's not, *over and over* — especially me.

Last week, I had some decent news that degenerated this week (just like my hip apparently). Add that to someone saying, "You'd be healed if you had more faith," and my brain practically burst into flames. Yep — it made me that sad-angry. Flames. Flames. No one wants me to be healed more than me. I have kids.

So, let's find what I can be happy about today despite *trying* circumstances.

I'm gonna look at the bad and twist it positive. Sound good?

No. 1 – Immunotherapy infusions are not as fun as they sound. They make me tired and nauseous for about two weeks after. And now I have to do this every six weeks. *slow motion voice* EVERY. Six. Weeks.

My answer: Do your worst, cancer (*okay that's too bold*). Let's try that again.

Try me, cancer! I've given birth to five babies. I know how to deal with nausea and tiredness. Give me a bucket and a bed—I got this!

No. 2 – Once again, the doctor said there's no cure for my cancer, and they're just trying to stave it off for as long as they can, hoping to find a cure.

My answer: "Hoping to find a cure" means there's hope. And guess what. Even if it doesn't work out, the most I have to fear is death, right? It's always nice to know what we're facing.

If I had to randomly die tomorrow or be able to plan for it, well, call me a planner. That's much better than being taken out by a semi. Or a mountain lion. Or something.

No. 3 – They found another growth/tumor in my shin.

Um, how to make this good?

My answer: It's an excuse to not run a marathon, which one of my friends in Utah kept trying to pressure me into before I had cancer. I *suck* at running. In fact, I speed-walked Ragnar—and that was tough. Now I can get out of marathons and maybe even doing the dishes. One point for Elisa. Bing!

No. 4 – The last (terrifying) thing.

My bone and muscle are showing slight degeneration in my right hip.

My answer: At least I still have two hips. *Bam!* So what if I'm slowly falling apart. I've watched Monty Python: "'Tis merely a scratch!"

I have another MRI on Friday. After work, I'll be traveling back down to Utah again.

The only moment that is/shouldn't be funny happened when my son heard about the degeneration of my hip—and he immediately said, "Are they gonna be able to save it?"

"Save what?" I asked naively because I hadn't yet gone to *the worst* possible outcome.

"Your leg? Are they gonna be able to save your leg?"

"Good, Lord—that got dark fast! They might do radiation on my hip. But I hope they won't lop off my leg just yet." Then I broke out laughing, so grateful that I have a leg—two of them, in fact.

And he laughed too. "Sorry, Mama," he said. "I'm so glad you can keep your leg. Remember that pirate from Blackfoot?"

"Yeah. The guy who owned the gun store. The man with only one leg?"

"That's him. I guess you'd be all right if you ended up like him. I always did like that guy."

That's the spirit. I *could* end up like that ornery pirate in Blackfoot, Idaho. Yes! No matter the outcome, it's all coming up roses.

Call me a Pollyanna if you want. It's better than being bitter about everything, walking around dead when I clearly have so much livin' to do.

Merely a scratch, a flesh wound. It'll be all right.

CHAPTER 17
Always More

We all have secrets. I glanced around the hair salon. What baggage do those people have?

"This is the hardest thing I've ever been through!" a beauty said, her luscious hair swaying.

My ears perked. My religious friends say that loving gossip—and eavesdropping—is bad. I'd make a terrible Catholic.

"My favorite restaurant closed." Mrs. Luscious almost whined.

Um, seriously?

"I haven't known anyone personally who's gotten COVID," she told the hairdresser in booth two, "but it's been terrible to be quarantined with *my* children *all* the time! My husband and I can't even go out dancing to our favorite place anymore!" She paused to appraise herself in the mirror. "Did you hear the schools shut down on Friday because so many teachers were sick?"

I wanted to flip out on Mrs. Luscious and tell her what bad things actually are, how I could die soon, how I can't dance ever again because of tumors. How my son died! Or how I'm *happy* to be quarantined with my children because it means I'm still alive and so are they.

I turned to my daughter and raised a brow.

"Okay," Indy whispered, "I know what you're thinking. But just because we've been through a lot more than she has, we shouldn't judge her. Maybe she *really* loved that restaurant."

I scoffed. Out of the mouths of babes. My kids are so great. I wanted to be a better person then, really. Yet, I couldn't stop imagining Mrs. Luscious in a horror movie. You know the character who's wearing a bikini, screaming and running around because they've never seen a zombie before, and you're trying to get them to calm down and fight, but they're too busy bawling about some dumb thing (like their favorite restaurant). Of course, they're the first to die.

"El... lyssia Ma... goog... ma?" Talk about a slaughter. I don't correct people anymore.

"Right here," I said and hobbled back to get my hair trimmed.

I'm embarrassed to say that I judged the hairdresser too. She stood perfect and darling. She's probably never experienced anything bad.

"Your hair is... interesting. It has a different texture in some spots, and the color is totally different too, blond, red, gray."

"I have cancer," I said in almost a monotone because I've said it so many damn times to about a million different strangers. "Huge chunks fell out from radiation, and it grew in differently."

My daughter stared at me, practically willing me to be my happy, normal self.

"I'm so sorry. I would've had no idea," the beautician said.

"It's okay." I smiled at my daughter. "Now it's growing out into a mullet! I told my kids first I got cancer and then I got a mullet. I don't know what's worse."

The woman broke out laughing.

"I lost my eyelashes for a while too! It's funny the things they never tell ya about. I'll admit that was pretty bad."

"Are you still getting treatments—I mean, are you getting better?" Her hands shook and her eyes glassed as if a memory had overtaken her thoughts.

I instantly knew that flawless beautician has experienced loss. And it must've been from someone who died from cancer.

"I'm still getting treatments," I said more gently now. "They initially gave me two years to live, and now they're saying I might have more."

The pansy in booth two—Mrs. Luscious—shut her mouth and started listening. She'd make a bad Catholic too.

The hairdresser told me everything then, how her mom died of cancer at a young age, and how her dad is fighting now.

She pulled up the sleeve of her right arm.

"Always more," I read the vibrant watercolor tattoo. "What does it mean to you?"

"We all have secrets," she said, mirroring my own thoughts from earlier. "There's always more to everyone's story."

Everyone on that side of the salon quieted down.

"My brother died of cancer," Mrs. Luscious said. "We used to get coffee together every morning. I'd go to the restaurant alone for years after he passed. But now, well, it's closed down."

The beautician finished my hair, and I went to pay.

"You've given me a lot more than a haircut today," I said. "I needed that reminder. There really is always more."

CHAPTER 18
Bread Crumbs

You know the feeling: you buy a car and suddenly notice that same car everywhere. Well, that's happening to me, but with cancer. The Frequency Bias (or Baader-Meinhof Phenomenon) has become quite disturbing, and I'm hoping my bias for noticing this everywhere will stop.

Despite my hopes, it seems like every movie I watch has some tragic end or features a side character who's fighting cancer. I even watched *Tenet* (an action-adventure), hoping to get away from the cancer theme, but then a villain randomly has (you guessed it) cancer at the end of the film.

I read a smutty romance last week, with a cowboy, a damsel, and cancer. I turned to newspaper articles and shorter stories, but those too are about cancer. *And* I've been getting emails from drug reps pressuring me to try their "cure for cancer." I really wish those sharks would leave me alone.

I had yet another MRI on Friday to see if I need more radiation on new tumor sites they found. The whole thing felt so different. After they made me change my clothes and leave all my jewelry behind, I felt extra bare. The MRI machine felt even more like a coffin, the perfect metaphor for death.

I stayed in the machine for an hour and fifteen minutes because they ended up doing two scans after finding something in my back.

As the machine whirred around me, I thought of leaving my worldly belongings behind, like I'd just done in the changing room. When you strip me of everything: my ability to play the violin, my health, my love of writing.... When you get to the essence of who I am, I just wonder if I'll be good enough to spend eternity wherever God is.

The MRI finally ended, and it was a good thing because I'd been fighting a panic attack. As I collected my things and dressed in regular clothes, I thought of how it's time to breathe and find some semblance of equanimity. I might be seeing cancer everywhere, but I think it's really just because I'm scared. I'm not scared in the traditional sense (not right now anyway). I'm scared of the suffering. Going to treatments every six weeks. Enduring radiation. Possibly even more surgeries.

This is a fascinating study on America's preoccupation with preserving life. If we're not producing movies, books, or newspaper articles about it, we sure are talking about it over coffee: fearing the inevitable. Why? Since when did something so natural become villainized to this extreme? No wonder, deep down, everyone is so scared. Instead of being willing to embrace death when it's time, we continue fighting, spending every dime we have to stave off something all of us will experience anyway. Yet, I'm doing the same thing because more time with my family *is* priceless.

I just want to see all my kids turn eighteen.

I'm not shooting for the moon. Not really.

***

I was lost at the picnic. Droves of people weaved past, making me feel minuscule—insignificant. Then I saw her.

The woman wore short brownish-auburn hair, a checkered apron, and the cutest smile ever. She parted the crowd easier than Moses parted the Red Sea, and I giggled when I spotted her! My grandma—that tricky possum—ran toward me and clutched my hand. "You don't need to be scared of them," she said, motioning to the crowd, "or of the future. It's all been figured out."

And as soon as I saw her, I wasn't scared at all because, well, I wasn't quite so lost anymore.

My grandma died over a decade ago, and we had so much to catch up on. I wanted to tell her all about my kids and our lives. Relay to her how hard it's been being sick, hurting so much, and watching everyone else worry and cry. I wanted to tell her that the thought of an early death is daunting because I don't feel like it's time to go.

As if she heard my quietest thoughts, she peered into my eyes with so much love, and whispered, "Now, you're gonna come here much earlier than you'd want to. But don't be scared, Elisa. I get to be the one to show you around and help you get used to things. That's why I'm here, to tell you I'm waiting. Don't be scared. I'm here waiting to help you."

I glanced at her apron again—something she'd always worn during her life—and with that vision slowly fading, I woke up.

I tried describing the dream to some friends, but they didn't get the same peace I did. "Let me get this straight," one said. "You dreamed about a ghost who said she's just waiting for you to die. Oh, but it's okay because?"

"Well, that makes it sound creepy. It wasn't creepy. It was peaceful. Happy. She's my grandma, not just some ghost!"

Anyway, life can be so weird, how we lose people, but many of us somehow know we'll see them again.

I've been thinking about that dream for over two months. I thought about it today. The doctors did an MRI and found something the CTs couldn't display. The tumor in my tailbone has tripled in size, and they might need to do yet another surgery. I'm just starting to really walk after the last one, and this is a blow. The debilitating pain comes with worries that I'll endure surgery after surgery until I'm gutted like an Alaskan salmon.

Today, while waiting for the call from the doctor, apprehensive at best, my mind drifted to the dream. I could almost see my grandma again, and I smiled that she'd been wearing that checkered apron in the dream. She loved God and her family, but what she loved next seemed to be decorating, cooking, *and* aprons. I'd just been thinking about that when my little girl came into the house with a huge package.

"Some mail came. It's for you!" Indy waited excitedly as I opened the box, and when I opened it, I cried.

I swear I have the greatest family and friends in the world, and somehow—no matter how tough life is—they always make things better. My Aunt Colleen, Uncle Verlan, and their daughters had sent a care package with sweet notes, dish towels, and a homemade apron.

I immediately donned the orange apron. I imagined my grandma smiling down on me, telling me not to be scared of sickness or death. I slipped my hands into the pockets and found a paper inside.

"This was from an article Grandma Stilson cut out of a newspaper many, many years ago," the note said, and below was a story about (you guessed it) aprons.

I cried again, huge tears that wouldn't stop. I just couldn't believe my family had taken the time to do something so thoughtful — something so timely.

I never got the call from the doctor; they'll probably call with the news tomorrow. But I'm not as worried today.

These moments are my breadcrumbs from God. Whenever I'm feeling lost, I look for the breadcrumbs God has left in my path. They always lead me straight back to peace. To Him.

CHAPTER 19
Channel 6 News

"This is Julian Paras," the voice said on the other end of the phone.

"Hello." I didn't know what to say. Was this seriously Julian, the local news anchor?

"Someone called the news station and said we should do a story on you. Your blog hit a million views?"

I gasped. "Yeah. It did."

"Well, that's quite an accomplishment!"

I've been on TV and radio before to talk about infant loss awareness, but never just to talk about my blog.

"What do you blog about?" he asked.

"It originally started with random acts of kindness. I'd help other people and then strange miracles seemed to happen in my own life. But now that I have cancer, I'm writing a lot about those experiences. Trying to find the good in them."

I heard him take a deep breath. "I'm sorry. I didn't know. Well, would you have time for me to interview you at your house tomorrow afternoon?"

"Sure!"

I got off the phone and nearly screamed with excitement. I told Mike and the kids, and they were just as excited. They actually cleaned the house and helped me pick out clothes for the next day. We scoped out places where Julian could sit. Then they asked me mock questions, and we all laughed, making up ridiculous answers.

"I think this is awesome," Ruby said late that night. "You've had some bad things happen. I'm glad this is something good."

I tried not to shake the next morning, but I was extremely nervous. The kids and I plastered my hair to my head, just trying to cover the main bald spot. I spiked it weird in the hopes that it wouldn't show my scalp on camera.

Trey raved about how proud he was that "Mom would be on TV."

"Do you think we'll be on TV too?" He seemed a bit nervous. "I mean, our family picture? Kids from school might see it. No one at my middle school knows you have cancer. I just don't want them feeling bad for us."

I nodded. "I can totally see where you're coming from. Do you not want to be on TV?"

He must've seen the concern on my face. "I guess it would be okay if they know now. I can be on TV, Mom. I'm sure you'll talk about us. You always talk about us."

I hugged him so big; this was a concession from my shy little boy.

Indy helped with my makeup before she went to school—and Mike thought it was hilarious since preteens these days enjoy way too much blue eye shadow.

After everyone left for the day, I touched up my '80s-looking makeup and even tried some new permanent red lipstick that was supposed to stay on twenty-four whole hours.

It seemed like an eternity later when Julian knocked on my front door. He carried all sorts of things with him: a huge video camera, a stand, lights, a big bag with recording devices, and notepads. He nearly dropped his bag when he reached out to shake my hand and asked about how I felt that day.

"Oh, great," I said. "A little nauseous and tired, but that's just life with cancer. You get used to it."

We talked for quite a while as he stood to the side of the video camera. And after a minute I forgot what he was even there for. "Can I watch you work?" he asked.

"Okay? Yeah, I can show you my blog." After we visited some more, I told him how I've been playing my violin for cancer patients, and he even asked if I could play a song for him too.

But right before he left, disaster struck. "Oh, ma'am. I just noticed something."

I turned to him, growing paler with each moment.

"You have lipstick all over your teeth."

"Oh," my voice dropped an octave, "no. But you've been here all afternoon. How bad is it?"

"Well, it's not good. But I can edit it out. No problem."

After he left, I looked in the mirror and could have died. My teeth oozed of red. I looked great—with my mouth closed, but how had the twenty-four-hour lipstick gotten so grossly out of hand?

My phone buzzed. "Hello?" It was my boss from when I ran the newspaper.

"Did they interview you?"

"Darlene? You're the one who tipped them off?" I could've hugged her.

"Yes."

"It was amazing—the whole thing. Except that I got lipstick all over my teeth. And when I looked in the mirror, I looked like the undead. It really was an interview with a vampire."

She laughed so hard that I couldn't help joining in. "It'll be fine. I'm sure you did great!"

That night, the family and I nervously congregated around the TV. "This is so exciting," Indy said.

Yes. Exciting. My children—and the state of Idaho—would get to see what I look like as a vampire. But as my story came on, it played out so much differently than I'd expected. And all of us, even Trey, ended up with tears in our eyes.

"Elisa maintained her blog for ten years after losing a son, and now after reaching one million views, she says being diagnosed with stage four melanoma has made this achievement bittersweet." Julian's voice narrated videos of me working and showing him pictures of my family.

"Oh, my gosh. There we are!" Trey's face lit with excitement, and I realized just how much he'd actually wanted to be on TV.

"You still have to find the good," my voice rose proud and strong, lacking any trace of sickness. And to my complete delight, Julian had made my teeth so white they could've lit any darkened room. "Whether you're dying or going through something terrible, you have to make the best of things. I've made so many friends in the hospital and seen life from different perspectives."

"Through her blog," Julian said, "people have begun reaching out to her, asking for advice."

Then things grew very serious, and we heard *him* asking me for advice—for how to help kids cope with cancer.

"My kids have had a tough time," I said on-screen.

I turned to see more tears in all my family members' eyes.

"We've had some serious conversations with them about what the future looks like." Each of the kids' faces showed on the TV as I spoke, the camera scanning from picture to picture in our kitchen and living room. "I feel like we appreciate every moment, more than we ever have before."

Everyone came and hugged me in the living room at this point.

"Author of multiple books and her blog, Elisa says her achievements are nothing compared to making an impact to the people closest to her."

"All of these other achievements are great," my voice almost whispered from the TV. "It's astounding that I have a million views, and that my books are finally starting to sell. But it really doesn't matter if I haven't made a difference to the people who are most important to me."

We stayed there in the front room, a nest of a family, crying and then laughing at how hilarious we might look.

Mike turned off the TV, then Trey stepped away, acting like he needed to dust off his shirt. "That was pretty good," he said.

"I love you, Mama." Indy wiped her eyes.

And I have to say, seeing the happiness on my kids' faces made me feel better than I have in a long time.

CHAPTER 20
More Radiation

"You need more radiation," the doctor said, and my heart sank. The last time I had radiation, I threw up in front of my mother-in-law. *That* was embarrassing. Plus, radiation made me perpetually flu-like, caused hair loss, and gave me massive headaches.

"Well, at least it's not surgery," I said, forever an optimist.

"The neurosurgeon didn't think your body could handle another serious back surgery so soon. Radiation is the next best choice. Radiation and an adjustment to your treatments. Elisa, you might not want to hear this, but we need to double your dosage of medication and schedule your treatments more frequently. I know you were really sick before, and I hate to tell you, but this will be much worse."

I'd practically lived over the toilet for a couple of months after radiation in 2020. At least I know the drill and what it feels like to be a human pincushion. But for some reason, this news just struck me, and I'm mortified to tell you that I started choking up. Now that I need treatments every three weeks, it'll be extra exhausting and vomit-inducing. I'll be too tired to be a "fun" mom. It just sounds like hell.

I cleared my throat after the momentary weakness. "Like I said, at least it's not surgery."

The doctor spoke slowly. "You know, I've been reading your book, *The Golden Sky*."

"Wait, what? Really?" It completely took me off guard. And despite everything, I smiled. "What made you want to read it?"

"You're just so positive. I thought it would be fun to read about you. So, you were a homeless street musician?"

My face flushed. "Why, yes, I was." Did I have to put my whole damn life in that book? It suddenly seemed like a poor choice.

"Well, you're quite the writer. I feel like you're talking straight to me."

That busy woman had no idea how much her kindness meant to me. "I can't believe you're reading it. I'll never forget this. Ever."

"Elisa, about this cancer stuff, whatever the future holds, I know you're strong enough to handle it. You've made quite an impact on us at the hospital. And just know, we'll be reading about you."

I laughed so hard. "We?" I asked when I could finally talk.

"My nurse is reading it too."

After the appointment, instead of being totally discouraged that the cancer is getting worse and that I need more radiation and stronger treatments, I glowed. I couldn't believe my oncologist and her nurse are reading my book! They are so incredibly busy, and this showed a level of thoughtfulness I can't quite explain.

So, I have more intense treatments ahead, but my doctor helped me find something good despite the hardest of days.

CHAPTER 21
Funeral Directors and Fortune Tellers

I felt a bit hopeless yesterday—embarrassingly weak. It's just that the feverish feelings, nausea, and vomiting are getting overpowering. I just don't see an end to this fight.

I've started seriously studying Judaism, just as a way of coping. I'm currently reading three books, just devouring everything I can. And although I'm only studying, through its tapestry I've begun to sense a beautiful meaning in life. And when I felt so sad yesterday, a strange memory came to me as I studied.

A lady burst through the newspaper's dilapidated front door. She wore a fur coat to befit a queen. This really stuck out in Blackfoot, Idaho, which houses the Potato Museum, some excellent farmers, and various industry workers like welders, food production experts, and the like.

"Where's the publisher?" she boomed.

A couple of employees pointed to me, and the woman seemed shocked that I didn't sit in the big office behind me. Instead, I insisted on sitting in the main area with everyone else, because we all worked hard; we were *all* equal on that team.

"Hello," I said, standing to shake her hand.

"I do not shake hands. Don't you know who I am?"

"I'm sorry if I don't remember. Have we met before?"

Come to find out, we'd never met, but the woman had starred in numerous Hollywood films decades before.

I wanted to recognize her. She looked to be in her late eighties, and I could tell she needed to be known. I scribbled down her name, but I couldn't place it.

"I stopped by so you could write a story about me. We were passing through. But since you have *no* idea who I am!"

"I can still write the—"

She stormed from the office and left as quickly as she'd come.

I sat down, completely stunned. Everyone else had gone back to work, but the whole interlude shocked me. I Googled her name and, sure enough, found her in some song-and-dance kinds of films. Granted, she wasn't a Ginger Rogers, Debbie Reynolds, or Doris Day, but she'd been famous, beautiful, captivating... once. Now, she seemed forgotten in a world where younger generations had no idea who she'd been. Her whole sense of self-worth had been wrapped up in everything she'd lost.

As I thought about this woman from the past, that memory seemed so close to home. Not that I was a famous movie star (I wish!), but that so much of my worth has been wrapped up in my health. Who am I now that I take old-lady naps in my thirties? Things have drastically changed for me. But that doesn't give me the right to feel bad for myself or become so wrapped up in my past that it mars my future.

I'd read a book by Kirk Douglas, *Climbing the Mountain*, about how he found his way back to

Judaism. I wondered if he ever met that woman who came into the newspaper. Who knows?

In the end, what made life worth living for Douglas was simply giving to others, and that we should strive to live as long as we have the capacity to give. I so wished the woman with the fancy fur could read those sentiments. Maybe she could finally move on from the stardom that made her and later began destroying her from the inside.

So, yesterday after I rested for most of the day, I got up and tried to do an act of kindness for someone; albeit small, I wrote a note I knew would make a friend smile.

For a moment, the pain and everything abated. I thought about how I wouldn't trade anything for what I have right now: a chance at life, a chance to overcome and find good even in the pain, and finally, a chance to give. There's beauty in the journey, sometimes we just have to open our eyes a little bit wider.

***

Yesterday was weird. A funeral director called and left a message on my phone. "Hello, um, Elisa. I heard you were interested in hearing more about our services."

Funny thing. I didn't call that man. And I don't want to hear about his services. This came on the heels of three strangers' messages about miracle drugs that cure cancer. One drug is *only* $1,000 a pill—what a bargain—and all the sales reps who've contacted me through Facebook are incredibly pushy.

These messages were sobering in a way that made me sink with weariness. One of my friends thinks they're calling me after the TV interview. I've gotten an amazing amount of feedback on it. A man from NBC in Oregon even reached out to me.

"Do you think the funeral director heard about me from the TV interview?" I asked Mike. "Who would give my name to someone like that?"

He stared at me, stunned.

"I have no idea," Mike said, looking less stunned as his voice came out forced and his muscles pulled with stress. "Can I see your phone?"

He listened to the message and called the man back. "We didn't call you."

"But someone said you're interested."

"We—listen, we're not interested. We're just fine."

That was the biggest lie in the history of the universe because we really weren't fine, not that day. Sometimes this crazy fear grips me; maybe I should call a funeral home and just get an idea. Will my funeral cost $8–$10,000? How much will my family need?

I guess we all should think about this at some point, but I don't want to. Not yet.

Mike hung up the phone, and I looked into his big, blue eyes.

"We've had so many amazing people help us," I said. "We've received a tremendous amount of emotional and financial support. I shouldn't let this bother me. But that man, well, he was like some sort of human vulture."

Mike held me in his capable arms.

"I'm scared," I said after a moment. "The cancer is getting worse where they thought they took it out. I just want to know if I'm going to make it or not. I don't want to lose hope, but I need to be realistic."

Mike, that hilarious, strong man, said, "Sometimes... Elisa, well... sometimes I get scared too. I don't want to lose you."

Mike scared? That shocked me.

We stood there, fiercely holding each other just because a funeral home director had called, trying to make some money.

***

The woman was a modern-day Maureen O'Hara. She was so beautiful, people wanted to believe everything she said. She made it feel as if her clients had their fortunes read by a Disney princess.

I thought even if it made no sense, it would be memorable. But deep down, I hoped she'd be able to tell me something the doctors couldn't.

We sat among wavering candles and purple lights. She'd tacked blankets and bandannas all over the walls and beads hung, clinking from every doorway as the heater kicked on.

I had big hopes for this afternoon, and as she told us to close our eyes and breathe slowly, my anticipation only grew. The sounds of rippling waters invaded my sense as the smell of fresh lavender gilded the air. Finally, I would know more about my prognosis.

But instead of answers about illnesses and the future of my family, the reading went to a weird place. We were Scottish settlers who'd had many children who died. And we weren't married. But Mike and I had lived together in sin... long, long ago.

At one point Mike's grandmother even appeared in the room. This seemed odd because both of Mike's grandmothers are still alive.

"She wants me to deliver a message to you," the woman said in a creepy monotone.

"My grandmother?" Mike queried, nearly breaking the spell.

The woman must've realized she'd made a mistake because her eyes widened momentarily before taking on a glossy sheen once more. "Yes, your grandmother, from *two* generations back."

After the woman's eyes receded back into her head, Mike looked at me and raised a skeptical brow.

After we got in the car, he smiled. "My grandma didn't have to come all that way," he said. "If she wanted to talk to me, she could've just called."

"But this was your great-grandmother."

We both broke out laughing.

"You're not disappointed at all?" he asked. "You were so hopeful."

"I can say one thing. I'll never forgot it."

Plus, I learned something important. I need to stop looking for answers in the wrong places. Sometimes the people we should be reaching out to are only a phone call away. It shouldn't have taken a psychic to tell me that.

Next time I need advice, instead of seeking out strangers, I'll just call Mike's grandma!

***

Our dogs barked and ran in the basement while our white cat hissed frantically. I went downstairs, but it took me forever to get there because I'm still unsteady on stairs. And when I rounded the corner, I screamed.

Indy's brand-new kitten pawed at a beautiful dead squirrel!

I'm still not sure why I screamed. But after I did, Indy, stood by me, mouth ajar, and then she screamed too — in perfect harmony.

Trey rushed downstairs, his gaze bouncing from our vibrating vocal cords to the dead squirrel.

"So, it's... a... squirrel," he said. "So what?"

"A *dead* squirrel," I responded. Plus, the thing was as big as Indy's kitten! From its tail to its head, it stretched at least a foot and a half. "I've seen dead mice, and I can handle those now. But this is huge!"

"Dude, look at its razor-sharp teeth, too!" Trey said.

We were all a bit relieved when Mike finally joined the celebration of life and disposed of the body.

Ruby heard about the squirrel, too, and that evening all three of the kids wanted to talk about it at length during dinner.

"Well, death sucks," Indy said. "I've learned that from the school counselor. Plus, I think that was the cool squirrel we'd always see jumping from tree to tree in our backyard. Won't see that again now, will we? The counselor is gonna hear about *this* tomorrow!"

We've had to talk about death a lot lately. It's nice that the schools are trying to help the kids, but they come home with a lot of questions I don't know how to answer: "Why are you sick?" "How long will you live?" "Why would God let to us happen to you — to us?"

I investigated Indy's somber face and knew I had to think quick.

"Squirrel death!" I suddenly announced. "We each need to come up with a story of how it died."

Trey and Indy seemed immediately stoked about the idea. Ruby and Mike joined in, seeing through me.

We went around the table, and suddenly instead of it being this terrible thing, we started laughing so hard I could hardly breathe.

"It was a tragic romance. That squirrel died for love!"

"Well, I think it was a spy!"

"I *know* it's been living in our house for weeks."

And the stories went on and on. Living in Idaho isn't for the faint of heart. Now we've had mice, a raccoon, and a squirrel in our house.

Hopefully, the kids will never forget the day we tried figuring out just exactly how Bucky the Squirrel died. Personally, I think it was a mob hit. You should've seen that face—he looked like he'd been up to no good!

CHAPTER 22
Sunday of Life

I haven't had a fairy-tale life, but as I look back, there are numerous moments that shine with pure magic. I might share those someday, write them down so my family can know a little bit more about me and remember the good times. Maybe....

The relationship with my second oldest daughter, Sky, is strained after she ran away. She's still living in Utah, and I worry she doesn't fully understand how much I love her. She doesn't understand much about me actually. This might sound inconsequential, but it's important to me. The doctors say time could be running out. If my words are all she has to really remember me by during this time, well, at least she'll have those—if she ever wants them.

Right now, I know I need to be forgiving even though it's much easier to feel hurt. Being a teenager is hard. They think they know everything, and it's awfully tough to look beyond that. After all, I ran away at seventeen so I could be a homeless street musician in Hawaii. When I wasn't cold and hungry, I had an absolutely amazing time fiddling, but I didn't think of what it had done to my family back home.

All of this reminiscence and regret again because I talked with a different doctor last week. The conversation still has me reeling. Once again, some specialists had hoped for all the cancer to be eradicated in some areas, but it's not. To top that off, the tumor in my tailbone is still growing. My regular doctor hadn't fully relayed the import of this news, and when this different man spoke with me and Mike last week, although I appreciated his honesty, his words made it hard for me to breathe.

He talked about the melanoma in my brain and how all sorts of things could happen out of nowhere. The "coulds" went on and on—and on. In fact, at the end of the conversation, he urged me to write a will.

"I met you in the hospital," he said.

I felt embarrassed, but I couldn't remember him. Parts of my one-month stay in the hospital are still a blur.

"I remember how much everyone liked you there. You're just so happy and innocent-seeming about everything. They still talk about you—and how you played the violin for the other patients. How happy you were even after surgery. And even now your doctors have spoken highly of you."

"Thank you," I said, but I wondered where the conversation was headed.

"But."

There it was.

"I don't know if they've talked candidly with you. It's hard when you like someone so much—and they seem so happy. You don't want them to hear the worst and lose hope. You don't want to be the person to break the spell. But I feel like you need to hear it. Right now, you're active again. The point is that you need to be prepared. Unless something very unexpected happens, you know what you'll die from."

I had heard this so many times. I remained strong for the whole appointment, but later I descended into a deep depression that lasted for days. I know I need to think about death and how I'd like to live if I do need life support or something else. But it's still hard to fully comprehend that I'm the one in this situation. Not some stranger, distant family friend, or older acquaintance. Me. And I must make difficult choices right now.

I ended up calling a friend. He's a tall cowboy who you'd never expect to be a lawyer. He and his family—mainly his epic wife—taught me how to inoculate cows for an article I wrote for the newspaper.

I made an appointment with him. I said, "If I have to do this, I might as well have a legend draft my will." Nothing can be normal when I'm involved.

This took a lot out of me, but we'll just add it to my list. I've done some crazy things throughout this experience. I sent a letter to monks in Brazil asking for prayers, ordered these strange mushroom vitamin supplements that are supposed to cure cancer, saw a psychic, started attending the Baptist church again, studied Judaism, and talked to all sorts of specialists about what they offer across the world.

Something's gotta work, right? But if it doesn't, it'll still be nice to have a will that was drafted by a legend.

When you find out you might die, everything sort of stops. You stop taking Italian lessons, stop buying dresses that you might only wear one season, stop planning for retirement. You just quit progressing for a minute.

It hit me today how I need to start planning again. Sometimes when the work week is over and we've reached Sunday, I so dread not seeing the family on Monday, that I ruin Sunday. If this is truly the Sunday of my life, I don't want to ruin it. I want to really live.

***

"Can you lie on the exam table for me?"

But it's not a typical exam table. It has a huge body pillow on it, and the table is built to slide in and out of the CT machine.

The techs and nurses start forming the pillow around me, and as they push, the tiny beads inside begin to harden and bond together.

I start shooting the bull with the team during the process, telling them how I wrote an erotic novel that was finally published traditionally. For some reason they think that's funnier than hell because I "look so innocent."

"Those are the ones to look out for." I giggle the words. And I realize all our laughter makes this whole thing a little less terrifying.

"We have to remove your gown now," they say, and I unceremoniously hand it over. So many people have seen me naked in that place, I hardly care anymore.

The team pulls a plastic bag around the legless table, over my feet, and then up to my ribs. "This is a suction technique we use to immobilize patients during back radiation."

"I promise not to move." Was the vacuum seal necessary? I mean, I'm not a spastic toddler anymore. And I've been through this drill enough times that they should know I've gotten good at it.

"It's nothing personal. But this is gonna get tight. Ready?"

I nod before she flips a switch and I become like a human sandwich in a Food Saver bag.

The lights dim, and the table starts moving me in and out of the machine for about a million years (actually forty-five minutes). And despite my vast amount of experience with this, I suddenly get so scared that I tell myself this is a spa treatment, and I'm gonna be so toned afterward. *Want cancer AND abs, try this thing out!*

But soon it's too damn tight, my arms are practically glued to my sides, and I'm struggling to breathe normally from all the anxiety.

I slam my eyes shut, trying to remember something good because being vacuumed in a CT machine was not on my bucket list.

And then I remembered something that fully took me back in time:

The closest I've even come to touching heaven is when I fell from it. I didn't dive or jump, I simply leaned out of the plane, right before the wind took me. As I hurtled toward the earth, a feeling of freedom completely replaced all the fear I'd felt moments before.

The wind rushed past, and my stomach jumped into my throat, but only then could I truly see the beauty of the world. I looked everywhere, completely amazed by God's creation. The waters glistened, and the mountains seemed far more monstrous and impressive than ever before. I should have been more terrified than any other moment in my life, but time just stopped.

After seconds seemed to turn to hours, my tandem instructor pulled the parachute's ripcord. And I remained amazed, thinking about God and this great gift I'd been given. It astounded me that God created such brilliance and beauty. Yet among all of that, He'd somehow seen fit to create me.

That's what I thought of in the CT machine: how being scared of death can truly bring us to life.

CHAPTER 23
Layton Funk

I browsed Facebook one day and found Layton Funk's profile; although a complete stranger, he seemed inspiring and interesting. We started talking and eventually decided to meet up sometime. But meeting someone in person is always so much different than talking online, and I felt nervous.

When I entered the building, I mentioned who I'd come to visit, and everyone around raved about Layton.

It took quite a bit to see him though—COVID-19 has still put so many obstacles in everyone's lives. Both wearing a mask, Mike and I had to wash our hands for the appropriate time (as someone watched us), then we donned plastic gowns, took a COVID nasal swab test, washed our hands again, sanitized, then waited behind a glass screen.

"I'm so excited," I told Mike. "He seems so awesome online."

Then Layton simply rolled into the room, and I immediately smiled. He joked with us right off the bat, being far wittier than I expected, and the hour-long conversation that followed had moments I'll never forget—he even let me play my violin for him.

Layton has quadriplegia. He was in a car accident in Idaho over a decade ago, and now he lives in Utah, where his entire staff has fallen in love with him.

We talked about everything from his identical twin, our love of superheroes, board games, and his advice about how to handle terminal cancer.

We were told to stay behind the glass, but at one point Layton talked about his room. So, we repositioned the straw he blows in to move his chair, and he broke us out of jail, leading us on a secret mission to his fortress of solitude.

"Just act like you own the place," he told us, grinning.

We strutted past the desk, like nothing was amiss. The staff didn't even look up — and we actually reached his room. I guess that's just what happens when someone like Layton leads you on an adventure.

The man has an *entire* walk-in closet filled with the greatest superhero collection known to man.

"Holy crap!" I whispered. "This is... awesome." It was like entering Narnia, but different because I saw a bunch of Superman figurines instead of Mr. Tumnus.

We sauntered back to the meeting area — with the glass barrier — and this time someone from the center followed us.

At the end, I asked Layton how he does it. He had a completely normal life until the accident. I just couldn't imagine what he'd gone through over the years. This handsome man was still young and had endured unfathomable trials.

"I've been able to help so many people through this. It's my purpose."

My lip quivered because I've never met someone that positive and strong. He went on to explain how life can bring the strangest miracles even if they don't seem "good" at the time. His eyes sparkled when he spoke. For me, the world changed. I still couldn't imagine that kind of strength, but I was proud to know someone who did.

"I'll come back! We'll play board games." I promised, *but* that doesn't mean I'll let him win.

Even after Mike and I left, I couldn't shake the experience. Layton completely inspired me. His positivity and kindness were humbling. I could hardly wait to get back there so I can beat him at Monopoly.

***

I'd recently turned eight years old, and despite my mom's best efforts to keep me safe, that day didn't go as planned.

I always found strange refuges where I would hide, read, and imagine. My Greek neighbors—in their eighties—would visit with me and feed me tons of braided cookies.

They didn't know it, but when we weren't visiting, I loved to hide in the bushes at the side of their house. The plants grew so thickly together that I had to crawl just to get between them. I'd push through branches and spiderwebs, then lean against the brick house and read. The sun shone perfectly through the branches and most of the time my little black cat would join me. It became my own entrance to a magical world where I could escape and imagine.

That day I didn't read though—and my cat didn't join me. I thought about my friend, Candice. Days before, our moms had brought us to pick asparagus, but Candice seemed all wrong.

"I fell on the ground," she said. "It was a really hard fall. They had to rush me to the hospital. And I got cancer."

Cancer was previously unknown to me, and it sounded terrible. In fact, I never wanted to get cancer, and I never wanted to fall on the ground because that's obviously how people contracted the disease. Candice seemed so tired when she talked about it. Tired and sad. She said she might die someday, that we'd all die. I knew that, but I didn't want to think about it.

My magical place didn't seem so magical at the moment. I didn't want to stay there, thinking about how my friend might close her eyes and never open them again.

So, I crawled from the bushes, got on my scooter, and zoomed up and down the sidewalk. I'd sit and straighten my hands up so I could hold the handlebars tightly. I'd gone down a hill and was picking up speed when my old, Greek neighbor got into his car. It all went so fast. I tried to move, but the puke-green car sped too quickly, and the bumper slammed against my forehead.

I sprawled, my scooter screeching across the pavement. I hit the ground so hard, but I was shocked beyond tears.

Then my neighbor stood over me, screaming. "Oh, my God! My God!" His hands pulsed, up in the air. "I almost ran you over. I almost—"

I couldn't hear him after that. I'd fallen now, fallen hard just like my friend.

A few days later, my mom spoke with the man.

He claimed he could have killed me. He said he couldn't sleep anymore—could hardly live with himself. "I couldn't see her."

I really thought about death then. It was so strange to think about something I couldn't begin to understand.

My poor neighbor was strained after that. He and his wife gave me more cookies than normal, but he wouldn't meet my eyes for long.

I walked out of their back door one day, crawled between the bushes, and wished he'd never hit me with his stupid car.

I never saw Candice again, and I stopped visiting my neighbor. It was just too hard to see all that fear in the old man's eyes.

***

Several months ago, I received something quite unique in the mail: an envelope with a single feather in it. I later discovered that Mato-Uste had sent it to me after performing a smoke ceremony "around the campfire to contact the Grandfathers." It took a moment for me to understand, but he kindly explained that the feather was waved over smoke to help it soar to the heavens so the Grandfathers could bless and embrace me.

"You can keep the feather or release into the wind with a prayer. It will find the Grandfathers." Mato-Uste gained his wisdom about this from Mae Taylor—a highly respected Nez Percé holy woman. I love this man dearly, and his excitement about the feather made me happy. "The Grandfathers, Wolf Brothers, and Eagles will guard your passage. Be safe and happy."

My family members each expressed their curiosity about the feather. A couple of them told me to keep it.

"I don't know why," I replied, "but I want to let it go someplace special. It'll be a sign that God is listening to my prayer."

My brother thought of the perfect place. Windy Point features three cliffs that people can easily walk to. We drove there, and I struggled a bit as the car jolted along the bumpy road. But that was the least of my worries; I didn't know if I could even walk the short distance to the cliffs.

After we arrived, the sun shone brightly, showcasing the beginnings of spring. Plus, the area really lived up to its name.

"Hold my hand," Mike said, his hair blowing several directions as the winds shifted sporadically. "Are you sure you can do this?"

"I have to," I said. "It just seems important."

My parents, brother, sister-in-law, and Mike helped me slowly traverse the rocky landscape. We finally chose the cliff on the far right where everyone could stand around me in a circle. Then my sister-in-law gave the most wonderful prayer. Everyone backed away except for Mike — who held onto my waist. After enduring all these cancer treatments, the last thing I needed was to stumble off a cliff.

The wind blew hard, and I let go of that blessed feather. But after traveling away momentarily, it flew back — right to my brother. We tried again, and it boomeranged to my dad. We moved to another cliff that faced another direction and seemed more majestic than the last.

This must be where the feather wanted to be let go.

Defeating all odds, it came back again.

Completely dumbfounded — and even frustrated — my brother and Mike climbed to a cliff I couldn't reach. My brother let it go with so much ceremony in his face — and it came back. My mom even tried, but it didn't seem to matter who let it go, the feather always returned.

"It doesn't want to leave you," my dad said. "You should keep it."

Worn out, I had to sit on a rock before edging back to the car. As I sat there, something circled above me.

"Oh, my!" my mom said. "Elisa! There's a hawk above us!" And it was, glorious and perfect, glinting as it dipped and arced several times before floating away like I'd hoped my feather could have.

When the car disembarked from the canyon, I contacted Mato-Uste. "What does it mean?" The hawk had seemed quite amazing, but maybe it meant something else. Maybe God had rejected my prayer.

Defying my worst fears, the man said, "It's meant to be. The Grandfathers want to watch over you. I thought this might happen. You are blessed."

***

A few days later, my oncologist explained that several specialists had spoken about my case at the tumor board. "We're going to try a new immunotherapy," she said. "If it works, it could significantly extend your life."

A bit of hope glimmered for me. I've tried so hard not to be overly optimistic because I don't want to have my heart broken like when my son died. But still, maybe the feather staying really was a good sign. And these collaborative specialists could change the course of my life. Yes, the doctors dubbed that as an incurable kind of cancer, but the future might be brighter — and longer — than doctors originally projected.

We'll just have to wait and see, but until then, my feather is with me, reminding me of how powerful it is to keep hope alive.

CHAPTER 24
Confrontation

Sky texted me a couple of times recently. In the middle of the night—on school nights—which made me worry about her sleep schedule.

She's been getting terrible grades, even failing classes for the first time in her life. She had straight As when she lived here. Now she'll hardly talk to me, and I've been at such a loss.

I messaged her about this. "Your grades aren't great. I'm so worried about you. We miss you. I wish you'd just come home. I don't know what I did wrong, but we'll fix it. Sky, I'm worried about cancer too. I just want as much time with you as possible."

I didn't get a response until around midnight that night. "You've been a terrible mother. And I'm tired of your manipulative, pity-me behavior."

I stared at my screen and cried. "I'm sorry you feel that way," I texted through the tears. "Just know that I love you so much."

The words didn't even sound like Sky. Pity-me behavior? I'd heard of teenagers being tough, but this was a whole new level. How could she send messages like this while I was so sick? I turned off my phone and rolled over in bed.

It wasn't until the next afternoon that I called the "Interloper." He only sees the kids a couple of times a year, other than taking them to lunch on their birthdays. I wouldn't be seeing him for months, and I absolutely needed to make him talk about Sky.

"She's failing classes," I said. "She's never failed classes.

"She has a lot of problems, Elisa. I've never seen a more antisocial, depressed kid."

"Antisocial?" She could get sad sometimes, but I wouldn't use the word depressed. In fact, Sky has always been such a positive, happy source of light. People were just drawn to her, and she'd been voted class president a few years back. "You know, I don't think it's good for her down there. She really needs to come home."

He laughed. "Well, I disagree. I'm finally getting to know her."

"Those grades though."

"I told her she better shape up or she'll have to move back with you." He chuckled. "She seemed pretty shook up when I said that!"

My face heated. "Listen, I'm gonna level with you. I've obviously been the one to raise the kids all these years—me and Mike. You worked on your new relationship and new family. I worked multiple jobs as a single mom and have done everything I could for my family. And now Sky is suddenly with you while I'm facing a life-changing diagnosis?"

It felt like the story of *The Little Red Hen.* "The doctors have said what's helping me fight and get better are the kids. I'm fighting so I can be there *for* them— they make life better for me, and I make their lives better too. They need a mom. Sky should be here too."

I hadn't been this blatantly honest with him for a long time. And instead of responding rudely, the conversation shockingly turned productive.

"It's crazy you're sick," he said. "And I know your whole life has been raising the kids. I'll try to convince Sky to go up to see you sometime soon."

When I hung up, I hoped things would get better: that Sky's grades will come up, that she won't be sad, and that she'll ultimately come home.

***

A man on Facebook sent me a friend request with an odd message. "Hello. I've been praying for you. I'm praying you'll be at peace with whatever struggles might be going on in your life so you can beat cancer. I met your parents in Georgia."

My parents recently bought an RV, and now they've been traveling across the United States, getting to know all sorts of people in RV parks and resorts. I have received so many messages from people in Georgia, Florida, Texas, Colorado.

"I swear you bought that thing just so you could get half of the United States to pray for me," I told my parents.

They'd laughed and laughed. "Well, we have met a lot of great people."

My dad authored a book, *Daily Inspirations From a Modern PHILosopher*. When they aren't enlisting people into their prayer army, they're giving out his books.

Lately, when I've gotten down, they've been my happy thought for the day. I just imagine them traveling across the United States, and that image makes life pretty good.

I need to keep up my faith. With RV people across the nation praying for me, who knows what good things the future might hold.

***

We had to start a GoFundMe because of medical expenses, and someone reported it as fraudulent. The company put a freeze on the account.

I had to furnish proof of not only my medical conditions but of our bills as well for their review.

As if that wasn't enough, the Interloper—the person who was *hardly* in the kids' lives and then suddenly resurfaced last year wanting to be involved—has been spreading terrible rumors about me, about why they think Sky ran away. I didn't want to believe it. After all, in my last conversation with him, I'd been vulnerable, saying the kids are my reason to keep fighting cancer. But now this. That's like attacking someone who's already hurting, crawling along the ground, literally fighting for their life.

I got confirmation of the rumors in writing last week, and the revelation—and court paperwork—stung. The documents alleged that I'm "mentally altered" and that all of the kids should live with him.

Before radiation, as the techs prepared me to go into the machine, I told them about all of this.

"Don't worry," they said. "Unfortunately, we hear stuff like this all of the time. Ex-husbands and ex-wives—especially—can be the worst."

"Right?" another tech said. "We even hear about people getting served with divorce paperwork *right* after getting diagnosed with cancer."

I could hardly believe it.

The Interloper has decided now is the time to take my kids from me—after I'd been the one to raise them. Not just Sky. All my kids. Because I have cancer.

It's crazy that other patients go through similar things. But I was still in shock. As I got into the radiation machine, I fought the waves of nausea that rolled over me. And I wondered about the court paperwork and about who had reported my GoFundMe.

This experience has been hard enough; I couldn't believe I'd have to get a lawyer and fight to keep my children. I needed to find strength within myself that I wasn't sure I had.

I tried so hard to be the best mother ever. I wished today I could get some validation that I'd done a decent job.

***

I sound like a broken record, but I've been thinking about Sky again, just wishing she'd come home. I feel so rejected that she's stayed away even though I have cancer. Maybe I'm just a terrible mother. Does she know about the paperwork I got served? I tried to text her, and she responded in the middle of the night—around one in the morning. They were pretty mean texts, all about how I shouldn't tell her I'm sick and that I'm just trying to be manipulative.

I don't know if I'm having weird dreams because of all this stress or since I've been thinking so much about death. Regardless, this recurring dream meant so much to me.

We're walking along a beach, and I find myself holding his hand even though we haven't seen each other in years. I keep gazing up at him and smiling. "I've dreamed about this," I say, tears in my eyes.

"So have I."

We keep walking, for miles and miles. My hair is well past my shoulders, and it flutters as we walk. Bits of sand gather between my toes, too, and I would have giggled, but this moment calls for quiet — for peace. It's so chilly I use my free hand to pull a shawl closer to my shoulders. I should have fastened it with both hands, but I'd rather die than lose contact with him now.

After we've traveled a while, we both turn to the sunset. "It's beautiful," I say.

"And it brings a memory with it," he says, knowing more about me than any living person.

"Yes."

"Will you tell me?" he asks, like a child.

I nod. "Once, when I was very young, when colors seemed more important than a career, and playing the violin in a nearby cave was more desirable than anything, I said a prayer."

He smiles. "And what did you pray?"

I look out at the waves tumbling from miles away. "I asked God to give me a sign that He still loved me."

We remain quiet. I bathe in our silence and will the moment to never end.

"Did you doubt His love so much?" he asks.

"I guess I did."

I pause, wondering over the small moments that make up our lives. "Well, nothing happened for the entire day that I prayed. I painted and drew. I went to my cave and played my violin. At one point, I knelt next to a rock and so much sadness overcame me. 'God, don't you love me anymore?' I asked.

"The voice seemed still, small. I didn't hear it at first because it was just a nudge. But before long the words filled my very being, and I FELT them. 'Of course,' a voice replied, and the air smelled of incense. 'Look,' the voice said.

"I turned to the sunset and my breath stopped. It was unlike anything I'd ever seen. The clouds stretched orange and gold. They were stunning—my favorite color not because of its hue but because of its representation."

"What does orange represent, to you?" he asks.

"Eternity." It's a simple reply, yet I know he understands. It tells more about me—about the desires of my heart—than almost anything.

"How interesting," he says. "Eternity is what you long for more than anything. Some wish only for fame, fortune, or even death after years on Earth. You... seek eternal life." He pauses, still holding my hand gently. "And you knew God loved you because of the beautiful, orange sky? You thought he answered your prayer?"

"Yes," I say. "I knew He answered it. In some way, it made me realize how He painted the sky for me and for each of us, every single day. His love shines everywhere, through almost everything."

"And that's what you hold onto whenever bad things happen in your life?" He studies a shell by our feet, and I don't say a word. "You remembered that, even when I died."

I don't want to talk about his death, not when he's standing beside me. I need to answer his question though. He deserves the truth. "Not at first, but yes. I remembered that sky. I knew how much God loved me, and all of us. I couldn't lose sight of His answer to my prayer or the gifts God has given me each day of my life."

Zeke—my son—just nods. I can tell he's thinking hard about something before he breaks the silence. "I'm glad God picked you to be my mom."

***

Indy was out with Grandma Dee — showing off her mad scooter skills. She shot down a big hill and turned on the newly cleaned street. Seconds later, Indy ran inside, bawling, and I knew she'd broken her wrist by the coloring and how it bent unnaturally.

I rushed her to the hospital.

"Mama, can you hold me?"

Indy is eleven now, and she hasn't asked me to hold her for a couple of years. But I got onto the hospital bed with her and hugged her. She's so precious — all of my kids are — but this was just one of those moments I'll never forget.

We were at the hospital for over eight hours. During that time, we watched a romance on my phone, told stories, played one-handed Cats in the Cradle, and had fun doing anything else we could think of.

We'd been there for a while when the hand specialist finally came in. By this point, Indy was hurting badly, and little tears had started to fill her eyes.

"Can you tell me what happened?" the doctor asked, looking from Indy to me.

"Well, you see, we were swimming," I said, and Indy's eyes widened with confusion. The doctor pulled out a notebook and started writing things down. "When out of nowhere this huge shark barreled toward us! I thought we were goners! But not with Indy around." I gazed at her and grinned. "She socked that shark right in the nose. Tore its head clean off!"

Indy started laughing so hard the bed shook.

The doctor removed his glasses, a bit bemused. "I can't believe I started writing that down." He shook his head. "Now Indy, can you tell me the *real* story?"

"Yes." She giggled. "I went down a hill I've never tried before, and I fell. Then my brother said to get up and that I was fine. But I really think I broke my wrist."

He showed us the X-rays and explained that Indy would need to be put under so her could pop her bone back in and place a splint.

Indy bravely went into the room with the sedation team, and they let me watch through the window. I cried, tears seeping into my mask. But I'd told them I was brave enough to watch, so I wiped my tears quickly and regained my composure. Within minutes, the medical staff finished, and the ketamine began wearing off.

"Mama!" Indy cried. "Where are you? Mama?"

I shot into the room before they even told me I could, and I held her left hand. "You're okay, baby."

"It's all blurry. You have so many eyes. Everything's all wrong!" She sobbed.

The nurses nodded, deciding I could stay while the medicine wore off.

I pressed my forehead to hers. "Just close your eyes." Then I sang to her. It reminded me so much of when she was a baby, as she slowly calmed down and placed her arms around my neck. I tried not to get emotional again, but I just loved being close to my little girl. I sang to her for a long time and when I backed away, her eyes could focus, and it seemed that the sedation had fully lost its hold.

"I love you, Mama. I don't know what I'd do without you."

"I don't know what I'd do without you!"

It hit me for the millionth time how these moments are what matter in life. It's not the stupid things we use to stack ourselves against. We might try to measure ourselves with accomplishments, but the greatest accomplishment is when those closest to us know how much we love them.

Mike came to the ER as soon as he could, so worried about both of us. After hugging Indy, he turned to me. "How are you feeling? Are you okay?"

I nodded, stunned. For all that time I'd forgotten about the cancer, the pain, and all of it. I'd just been enjoying time with the precious little girl who can bring light into almost any situation.

CHAPTER 25
Prices We Pay

"Just two more years."

"Fine, but it'll cost you."

"Cost me what?" I ask, dubious.

"Only your left wrist. And you might never play the violin again. That's my final offer. Is it worth the risk?"

I look into his steely eyes. He's far less sinister than I expected, but regardless, I never want to see him again.

"Fine!" I tell Death, and I hold out my hand so we can shake on it.

Doctors remove the melanoma from my wrist, even a little of the bone too. But despite Death's warning, I learn to rotate my wrist a little differently, and I begin to fiddle again.

Two years pass before Death meets me again. He's always standing by a boat, always wearing a cloak that sways in a wind I can't feel.

"Two more years," I say.

"It'll cost you."

"Good, Lord! What do you want this time?"

"Just part of your spine. You'll never walk the same again. People will pity you — think you're a cripple."

"Pity?" I don't want to see people's pity. *But* I want to see my children grow up. "Will it hurt much?"

"Course it'll hurt!"

"Fine." We shake hands.

I undergo a surgery to have an entire vertebra removed.

And every several years the meetings continue until I'm a shade of myself, and I've lost everything except the desire to die, for it to all be over.

I wake up, sweating, feeling like someone stands beside my bed. I rub my eyes and realize it was just the dream again—the one where I bargain with Death. And I wonder what prices we're all truly willing to pay to keep on living. At the cancer hospital I see clearly what prices people have paid—and they see my price too.

CHAPTER 26
In God's Hands

On Saturday, the side effects from radiation got so bad I didn't know if I could continue treatments. It might sound pathetic and weak, but the only thing I'd really kept down for six days was an orange. And although I kept dumping fluids into myself, it felt like pouring water through a hole-filled bucket.

Finally, when things felt their worst, I crawled into bed.

"Are you okay?" Mike asked.

"I'm scared. I'm so dehydrated and sick. I feel feverish. If things don't get better fast, I'll need to go to the ER."

Mike brought me some food and a drink. I tried to eat slowly, but despite antinausea medications, my stomach already churned.

"Mike," I said, "can you please pray for me?"

Mike doesn't pray. But he did then — and it meant the world to me. After falling asleep, I rested in the fetal position in God's massive hand. I couldn't see anything other than His hand and the sky which He lifted me into. And even though I didn't have a blanket, it felt so warm and perfect. This strange energy flowed through every bit of me, simply filling me with resilience. Even in the dream, a strange thought came to me: that someday I'd be in remission.

This sounds crazy because all the doctors have said I have an incurable mutation of melanoma. Even if radiation and the new immunotherapy *do* work, they will only extend my life, not save it. Yet, there was this feeling... and an unimaginably beautiful dream.

That morning, I woke up stunned that I'd kept the food down. I sat at the kitchen table with Grandma Dee, who was visiting from Missouri, and Trey. I couldn't shake the feeling of lying in God's strong hand.

"Look," Trey said, pointing out the back window. Dee and I turned to see a huge hawk, perched on a branch about fifteen feet away, just staring at us. After it flew away, I tried drinking more water. Amazingly, it stayed down.

I'm trying not to get my hopes up, but that dream and its premonition have buoyed me through radiation this week. What do I have to lose anyway? Worst case, I'll be let down; best case, I'll see a miracle.

Regardless of what happens, I'm thankful to have a renewed faith in the future.

***

"Grandma," I said to my Grandma Stilson when I was in elementary school, "I keep going to church to get saved over and over."

My grandma was a different religion than me, and she didn't fully understand what I tried to convey.

"Wasn't once enough?" she asked.

"Maybe," I said. "But maybe not. I might just be bad, and that's why God is doing this to me. When I close my eyes, I can't make the words stop. I keep seeing stories in my head. I pray that God will save me *and* stop the words. He's punishing me for when I've been bad. That's why He's making me see the words."

She laughed so hard before trying to clarify. "Seeing the words?"

"On a keyboard," I said. "Someone's typing them."

It was always the same. I'd see these crazy hands typing more and more. A stupid red mug — with swirly paint — sat by the keys which never stopped clicking.

"Maybe it's you," Grandma Stilson said. "Maybe you're meant to be a writer."

It was my turn to laugh. "No. God is doing this 'cause I'm bad." Then something hit me. "If I *am* meant to be a writer, there's just one thing I'll need."

"What's that?"

"Someone who's really good. I'll need that person to teach me."

My grandma died a little while after that. She's the only grandma I'd known. Whenever I wanted to give up on anything, she would be there, wearing her beloved checkered apron, and cheering me on. After she passed, sometimes I found it hard to keep believing in myself as a writer.

I think that's why my grandma had to send me an angel.

Many years passed after my grandma's death. I picked up writing again and even hired an editor to perfect my fantasy novel. But after I sent her the payment in full, the editor pulled out of the project.

"Unfortunately, the payment was over a $1,000 worth of dresses I sewed for her daughter," I told a friend on the phone. "Reselling them would be a nightmare. It's just such a specific size. Plus, her daughter looks so happy in the pictures. So, I just let the lady keep them. I guess they're going through some hard times."

"Oh, wow."

"Yeah, but what am I supposed to do now? There's no way I can pay someone else."

After a small pause, the woman said with a hint of excitement, "I'll help you!"

At the time I had no idea who this woman really was. I'd only known her a short while. She lived in Missouri, and I lived in Utah. We'd met through blogging and had started an unlikely friendship.

Although her offer to help was extremely generous, I did feel a bit cautious. Everyone thinks they're an editor, but the truth is, the wrong edits can completely ruin a book.

"This is so kind of you," I said, then committed. "Okay, if you're sure. Let's work on editing my fantasy novel together." I would give this a shot.

It turned out the woman had been an editor for a big-name publisher, and she'd worked with famous authors. I didn't know she'd sold thousands *upon thousands* of copies of her book *A Cat's Life* — in multiple languages. I just thought she was a fellow aspiring artist, an intriguing ex-nun who'd left the convent decades before, and a previous professor (with a deep understanding of Latin) whom I adored for even taking the time to build a friendship with me.

The moment she embarked on the project, I recognized her level of expertise. I was the student from then on — with nothing to give. A decade later, I'm still learning. She started calling me every day. Early in the morning, she'd read chapters I'd written, and then at night we'd spend between one to three hours revising them together. I went from knowing little about writing to learning more than I'd ever hoped for.

Months passed like that, leading to a life-changing conversation I'll never forget.

"When I started helping you edit your book, I was amazed with how fast you learned."

I'd wanted to tell her I soaked up everything I could because that was my dream—having a mentor just like her to teach me.

She went on, believing in me more than I believed in myself. "I've read many, many authors. You really have something special."

"You're so good to me." I couldn't fathom her kindness. And as she spoke, I typed some of her words into my laptop so I could keep them forever. That's when I looked at the keyboard. My crazy hands typed more and more. Then I noticed the stupid red mug— with swirly paint—sitting by the keys that never stopped clicking. And I remembered the vision I'd described to my grandma before she died.

I tried to keep my emotions at bay, but it was so hard.

I stood, remembering my Grandma Stilson and how much I miss her every day. I felt such a loneliness then, a longing to have someone like her in my life again. She'd been *such* a wealth of knowledge.

"Elisa." My mentor, Dee Ready, paused. "I told a friend the other day you've endeared yourself so much to me. We started editing this and we were good friends, but now I feel as if I have a granddaughter."

I cried then, huge tears, because Dee felt like family to me too—she always had!

It's crazy how I thought God was punishing me as a kid. Turns out He wasn't. He showed me a piece of what was to come—to confirm that I was on the right path. And then, to top everything off, He let me meet someone who would change my life forever.

Dee—now known as Grandma Dee—has been close to us for over a decade now. She's come out to help me while I've struggled with cancer. She's helped take care of the kids. And she's shown me such an abundance of love.

I needed her in my life, and I think she somehow needed me too.

I watched her playing with Trey and Indy today, grateful I get to have this extraordinary woman in my life. I'm so glad she came out from Missouri to help us for a couple of weeks.

CHAPTER 27
A Real Live Angel

I entered the waiting room yesterday for my last day in this set of radiation. Soon after, three women came in and quietly watched TV. I can never be quiet, so after a moment I struck up a conversation.

"What are you in for?" I asked. It's no secret that we all have cancer; I just wanted to know which kinds they are afflicted with. "I have melanoma," I overshared.

"Forget what I *had*. I'm almost done," one woman beamed as she spoke. "I'm getting better!" But she sat in a wheelchair, and she later explained that she could no longer walk because of the surgeries she'd undergone to remove the cancer. As she spoke, I wanted to join in her joy, but I had a feeling that things weren't quite as good as she conveyed.

The next woman—with long, blond hair compared to everyone's shorn heads—had a not very advanced breast cancer and was getting treatments to solidify her full remission.

And the last woman remained quiet. Stoic.

Finally, I asked, "What have you learned from this?"

"That God is good," the woman in the wheelchair said.

"I'm a lawyer," the woman with Elsa's hair—from Disney's movie, *Frozen*—confessed. "I've just learned again that life sucks."

It wasn't long after that both the woman in the wheelchair and Elsa were called back for radiation.

When things had totally quieted down and the door shut, the third woman spoke. I leaned forward, grasping onto every word, but she was so terribly hard to understand. "You asked," she lisped, "what I've learned. I haven't really learned, but it's been confirmed that life isn't fair."

"You got that right!"

She continued to explain that the cancer started in her tongue, and she had to have some of it removed.

I blinked back the heat in my eyes because I suddenly knew why she'd been so scared to talk in front of the others.

"They're doing radiation on my neck now." She spoke slowly. "The cancer... has spread."

"I can't imagine what you've been through. I thought I'd been on one helluva journey!"

"But you don't look like there's anything even wrong with you!"

A male tech came and called my name. At that point I struggled to stand, and my back had been pulled so badly that I hunched over and tried to walk straight.

The woman gasped, surprised at how I walked. "Talking with you was the best part of my day," I said. "I'm Elisa."

"Sarah," she said, placing her hand on her chest.

***

The gong resounded. Another person had finished infusions. Dozens of people clapped despite the IVs in their arms, and I was sure most of us smiled under our masks. But I wondered if anyone else felt the same way I did. I might never get to hit the gong. I might never be done with stupid infusions. I might never... get... better.

I wanted to pick up the mallet and go hit it hundreds of times just to say I have. But I'm not a two-year-old, so I didn't.

I also kept myself from saying any of this out loud. My mother-in-law sat beside me as medicine dripped directly into my veins. And we really were having the best time playing cards, visiting, and laughing. I didn't need to mar that with a sob story.

A woman near us spoke to a nurse, her words drifting through the partition that separated us. "He's awfully sad. He needs to do this."

My ears perked with interest. Who was sad? Who needed to do what?

Then, a man's voice began singing songs from my childhood — spiritual songs that are hard to forget.

And as he quietly sang "How Great Thou Art," I wanted to sing with him, this faceless man who sat in another cubicle, and the desire mounted stronger than almost anything in the world.

But it seemed embarrassing to sing in front of my mother-in-law *and* more than fifty other people in the room. Sure, they couldn't see my face, but they would hear me.

"I'll be right back," my mother-in-law said as if discerning my thoughts, and when she walked away the man started singing one of my favorite songs in the whole world.

"Holy, holy, holy is the Lord God Almighty."

I held my mouth shut. I'm not even religious anymore. I go to church, and I love God with all my heart, but I don't believe most of the things they teach. And yet, I could not control myself. I breathed deeply. I didn't need to sing with this poor man. Why was the desire overpowering?

"Holy," my voice joined his. "Holy." The harmony floated atop his deep baritone—matching perfectly in thirds. He must've heard me because his voice swelled with strength. He'd been shaky and scared at one point, but now his song grew strong and majestic.

"Almighty God," the words just flowed. And as we got louder everyone in the room quieted and simply listened to a moment that will always resonate within my soul.

We sang several verses and as much as it had grown, it finally came to a quiet, beautiful close.

When we finished, a woman whispered, "Did you... did you... hear that voice singing with you?"

"You heard it too?" the man asked, dumbfounded.

And even though we're not supposed to bother other patients, I grabbed my IV stand, stood from my chair, and peeked over my cubicle. "It was me," I said, almost giggling.

A stunning girl of about twenty stared at me with the widest eyes. Her dark skin glowed, and she beamed under her mask. "That was amazing you started singing too. I can't believe you knew the words."

"Thanks for letting me join in. Hang in there, you two. This isn't easy." And although I couldn't see the man from my angle, I sat down as my mother-in-law returned to the room.

"I sang with him!" I gushed. "It was awesome!"

My mother-in-law laughed. She's the sweetest woman, so full of love even though I'm the most random person ever.

The singer and his guest must've left soon after because a couple of the nurses came over to me and said, "That man was so sad and scared. His daughter said singing always makes him feel better. And what you both did. Well, that is one of the neatest things we've had happen in the infusion room."

"I couldn't help myself. But next time, you guys need to join in!"

"I really wanted to, but I didn't know the words. And then I realized, nobody wants to hear me sing," one of the nurses said, laughing.

"Oh, but I do! So, get ready for it. I'll be back in three weeks. While all of you are singing, I get to play the gong!" I could just see myself going crazy with the gong while everyone sang.

It's probably my favorite memory so far from this crappy cancer business: the time I got to sing with a perfect stranger who found some unexpected strength right there in the infusion unit.

I still can't believe they momentarily thought I was a real, *live* angel!

CHAPTER 28
The Day I Stopped Believing

The kids love the little Baptist church we're going to. Although I don't believe Jesus is the son of God, Indy does, and Trey enjoys going to youth group. The pastor knows that neither Mike nor I believe, and he's always saying hilarious or thought-provoking things as we leave the church.

This Sunday was different though. "We have something for you," the pastor said.

"Really?" Mike and I asked in unison.

The pastor and a deacon led us to a back hallway, and they handed us a card. "We just want you to have this. No strings attached."

"You know we aren't Christian," I said.

"We know. We just wanted to help." As we walked back to the front of the church, we got into a deep conversation that closed with the pastor asking me a very serious question. "When did you stop believing Jesus is the son of God? And *why* did you stop?"

That night I sat on the edge of my bed. Mike and I opened the card and felt stunned to find ten crisp twenty-dollar bills inside. "This is so much for them to give." I knew the church itself had been in dire need of money to help fix their nursing room.

"We can get more groceries now," Mike said, and I felt such a flood of relief. We've taken so many recent trips to Utah that we'd had to cut big corners to afford gas. I'd even started making quite a few things from scratch just so we could save a little here and there.

"You know how the pastor asked when I quit believing in Jesus?" I asked. "I was wondering, when did *you* stop?"

Mike had an interesting story. The teachers at his local Catholic school and church even thought he'd be the next priest. "But in junior high I realized the idea of 'God' just didn't make sense to me. I guess I didn't ever stop believing in Jesus — because I'd never started. I just admitted that I don't know if I've ever believed in God." He sat down by me and held my hand. "What about you? Do you know when you stopped?"

"Yeah, I think I finally do," I said. "It just came to me this afternoon."

The memory has haunted me, crouching, making me feel evil at even a momentary remembrance. I took a deep breath and told Mike what had happened to me when I was an impressionable teenager, back when Christians who loved Jesus as much as I did performed an exorcism on me.

I wasn't legally married, and I made a mistake at the age of seventeen: I had sex. Leaders swore that a demon had been transferred to me during the act.

The lead exorcist, the assistant pastor, made me sit in a pea-green kids' chair. For a moment I wondered if I was possessed because people I trusted implicitly said so.

"Open your eyes, demon!" the assistant pastor repeated until he practically shook me, and yelled, "Open your eyes!"

My little heart quaked inside, so scared. The look on his face. The vein bulging from his forehead. None of this felt right.

"What's your name?" he yelled, tiny bits of saliva flying. He—and the rest of the group—seemed so excited. An exorcism. This was a big deal.

I told him my name is Elisa.

He grabbed me by the shoulders and leaned on me because the chair I sat in was so low to the ground. "I'm going to need everyone's help with this one," he said.

He kept asking for my name until his grip clenched harder, and my left shoulder hurt. Then everyone shoved their hands on me with *such* a mob mentality. I've never felt claustrophobic like that, but the whole room came in on me. I couldn't move. I started shaking when I realized my real name wasn't good enough. Of course, they thought the shaking was a demon.

"Self-righteousness," I yelled, and I'm mortified to confess that I actually went along with it after that.

"Hallelujah, Jehovah!" the bad-breath exorcist said. "I know there are more in there. Tell us your names!"

Other people joined in with demands, clamoring for a piece of me.

"I don't feel anything evil inside me, guys. I don't feel... anything evil. I want to leave!"

"Tell us your names!"

"Violence!" I yelled and tried standing again. "Rebellion! Suicide!" I would say anything to leave that claustrophobic room with the pea-green chair. They gripped harder as I went on and on, hoping I could finally discover the secret password to freedom.

A while later it finally stopped because apparently the demons had flown out the window or something. The exorcists left the room so they could call the main pastor, and I stayed, crying in that pea-green chair. I turned around and kneeled, begging God for help.

They had as much conviction as I did. But it was a different conviction. I made a mistake; I didn't think that made me possessed. We had all believed in Jesus — the same Jesus. And they had *all* turned on me. How could they believe something with so much conviction? Maybe that could make me wrong too?

***

Walk about half a mile and you'll reach this vast peak right before the trail dives into the most beautiful valley you've ever seen. There are sage hens, deer, rabbits, and moose! You might even see a mountain lion, if you're unlucky. I've been there plenty of times, hiking a few miles in until I reach a bubbling stream where I eat my lunch and pretend I'm a nymph. I've even played my violin there. Sometimes the forest mutes itself when I fiddle, and other times, when I coax soft melodies from my violin, birds have stared as if they've never seen a violin before.

Mike and the kids have gone with me, visiting this secret place. And we always have some strange adventure, like the time a deer almost ran into us or when we realized a moose had followed us the whole time.

But now that I can't hike to my favorite place, I've been dreaming about it. Last week I didn't know if I could continue treatments, so sick beyond words. But today is better because I have a goal.

It can be exhausting just walking to the mailbox. In fact, sometimes I have to lie down afterward and rest. And even though we're living from scan to scan, I've made up my mind. I'm gonna reach that peak again — the peak half a mile in. If I can get a cane, check the mail each day, then go to the mailbox eight times a day, well, I can persevere to that peak! I can't make it to my favorite place *yet*, but at least I can stand in the wind and look down on that gorgeous valley.

I'm determined, and baby steps are gonna get me there.

***

I decided to bring the kids to the Baptist church and then take them to get their hair cut. To a regular person this might sound like a simple day, but to me it's a huge endeavor. Driving the car means I can't take my pain medicine. And with cancer treatments, doing more than one activity a day is utterly exhausting.

When we left church, my back had stiffened from sitting in the pew, and there's this strange feeling that creeps in from where the tumors are. It reminds me of when someone has a festering wound, something they just want to slather with Neosporin—that's how the tumors feel inside of my body sometimes. Too bad nothing has been taking that feeling completely away yet.

So, I limped into the hair salon and passed a family that left as we entered. Two hairdressers, who didn't have clients at the moment, laughed and joked; another helped a patron toward the back of the shop. None of them had seen me, Trey, or Indy until one of them turned and sighed.

"Did you check in online?" the woman asked, giving me a once-over.

"I didn't."

She shook her head. "Well, you should have. You might have to wait for a while." And the way she said it, I felt like a huge inconvenience.

I stood against the wall. They'd taken away the chairs because of COVID, and after watching the two available hairdressers BS for a while, my leg started shaking from the pressure. I should have left then, but my kids have needed their hair cut for a couple of weeks.

I can do this, I thought. *I can stay!*

My thoughts wandered, and I thought again about being an inconvenience. What had the main beautician gone through to act the way she had when we'd come in? She'd had an incredibly busy day, and maybe she just needed a break.

But I'd finally gotten out of the house, I have cancer for crying out loud, and I did not need her attitude.

My thoughts turned to other things. Being a burden is something I've worried about my whole life. I want to make people's lives better, not worse. And now that I have cancer, so many people are worried. So many people have had to help take care of me, doing things I simply can't anymore.

After about five minutes, one of the women left with orders of what her coworkers wanted to eat. I thought the other woman might start bringing the kids back, but instead she began sweeping the floor — in slow motion. After another ten minutes, I finally couldn't take it anymore.

"How can I help you?" she said blandly after I'd limped to the counter.

What was her deal? What had I done to bother this stranger?!

My back suddenly turned to fire. It wasn't good that I'd stood so long without my walker. "Please! Take me off your waiting list." I hadn't meant for the words to come out that way, but my filter left when the doctor removed some of my spine.

"Well, you don't have to get angry."

I blinked. She had no idea how much effort it had taken to come to their store. No idea about the cancer. No idea how happy I'd been to finally do something on my own.

At that moment, a man walked in, and the beautician turned. "Did you check in online?"

"I did," he said.

"Right this way," she responded.

Trey's mouth fell open. "That was ridiculous."

Both of my kids headed to the door. As I limped out of the beauty salon with my children, I could have turned to a puddle on the tile floor.

***

I'm not sure if it's common everywhere, but in our small town, people often intricately paint rocks, and then leave them on each other's porches as a random act of kindness. Recipients will tag photos of the rocks online with #PocatelloRocks, and they genuinely seem to love showing off the artwork left by strangers.

Sometimes the rocks will have words like "love" or "calm." Other times they'll showcase pictures of anything from cartoons to landscapes to animals. The rocks are normally small enough to fit in your pocket, and they're so popular that nearly everyone I know in this area has heard about them.

We came home, exhausted from another trip to the hospital. A rock—the size of a small dog—was propped against our door.

"Oh, wow!" I gasped at the details and vibrant colors. "I've never seen one this big. This is amazing!"

"Is that our neighborhood?" Mike asked the kids.

Upon further inspection, we realized it was. You could see our house and the neighbors' houses painted on the rock. Each home looked whimsical and fun. But our house shone, special. Little musical notes floated from our chimney, finding themselves on a treble clef staff that wrapped around the perimeter of the rock — the perfect musical border.

Mike hefted the rock so we could see all of it, front and back. "It's a beautiful day in the neighborhood," Trey started reading the words someone had scrawled on the back.

"Because of neighbors like you," Indy finished the sentence for him.

"Who do you think it's from?" I asked Ruby later that night. "None of us know."

"I've been wondering that too. But I didn't even see anyone drop it off! Whoever it is, they sure did a good job painting it. And those notes look like they might be an actual song."

I hadn't even thought of that. But after inspecting the rock again, I realized she was right. The person who had painted it obviously took extra time placing the notes just perfectly on that staff.

The next day, I sat talking with the neighbor to the north of us. My life had begun revolving around this beautiful rock. "I just wish I knew who made this for us. I want to thank them."

She got a mischievous grin. "Well, *I'm* not the one who painted it, but I know who did. And those notes on there... well, they might actually be a real song. Maybe you should try playing it."

So, that afternoon Mike and I pulled out my violin and asked the kids if they could video us as I tried deciphering the notes from the rock. Mike had to hold it on his lap, since it's so heavy. But he said he'd rotate it slowly as I finished each section.

Indy began recording as Trey sat and watched. The notes came out tranquilly at first. I had no idea what the song might be until we reached the third measure. After that, the melody swelled inside of my chest, and the meaning behind the words shot through my heart and my fingers. I could hardly believe what song the artist had chosen: "You Raise Me Up."

The words empowered me as my bows skillfully danced across the strings. I thought of standing strong and braving stormy seas. My violin rose to new registers as I willed myself to "be more" and totally trust in God's will. Mike and the kids must've realized which song I played at this point because the energy in the room completely shifted, and I knew we all felt the power of the melody *and* the meaning behind that song.

The last several notes brought a key change where the music flitted high above where it'd been before. My fingers danced across the neck of my violin with a quick grace that years of practice have afforded, and I grinned from the magic of it all.

I knew the song now and as Mike put the rock down, I let the harmonies overtake me. Then, I came to a quiet, resolute close.

After it ended, all of us remained completely still for a moment, lost within our own thoughts about what had just transpired.

"Could you tell what song it was?" I asked.

Both Indy and Trey nodded.

"You Raise Me Up," Mike said, smiling.

"Did you hear that key change?" I suddenly laughed. "When that came up, I didn't know if I'd make it!"

We posted the video online, and within a few hours it had thousands of views.

"She saw it," the neighbor to the north of me told me from her yard the next day. "The woman who painted the rock saw your video, and it blessed her heart so much it made her cry." She came and gave me a hug. "I saw it too. You played beautifully."

My neighbor had a strange sort of wonderment in her glimmering eyes. And I beamed as she spoke, knowing that the person who painted the rock knew how much their kindness had meant to our entire family.

***

Three weeks ago, I told my father-in-law that a strange peace overcame me along with the thought that I'll be in remission someday. I felt a bit embarrassed about that confession, until now.

"I have something for you to read and something for you to keep," he said after I got to his house. He left the table and came back with a faded envelope that read, "June 2007."

"You're only the second person to read this," he said, sliding the envelope across the table.

I held it gingerly — sacredly — since I knew this was important to a man I respected so much. After all, my dad and my father-in-law got me through my last rounds of radiation because I kept thinking about how they both had cancer and were brave enough to continue fighting so they could survive. That meant I better do the same.

I opened the letter and found it hard to breathe. It held the story of how a strange peace came to him once, of how during his darkest hour he somehow knew that one day he'd be okay.

I handed the envelope back.

"And this is for you to keep," he said.

Then, that softhearted Italian smiled as my eyes lit with wonder. "I carved it for you," he said.

My hands soon discovered every detail of the violin now in front of me, and a distant memory flooded my heart.

I was sixteen. The group had asked for a violinist to help them with a play.

"We'll tell the story," the woman said, "of a battered violin an auctioneer tries to sell. But no one wants it. And when the auctioneer is about to just give it away, someone steps from the audience and plays the violin to show its true worth."

They picked me to play the violin during this story. After I played, the auctioneer would get so many bids (from actors planted in the audience) that the worn violin would sell for thousands upon thousands of dollars. The show's patrons would marvel over the true worth of the violin in the story. In each showing, the audience always appeared genuinely enchanted as I played the violin and walked among them.

I thought of this play as I studied the little violin my father-in-law had made for me. And just when I thought I'd seen everything, I noticed a laminated note hanging from the bow. "What is this?" I asked, and then my breath caught because it's the story from the play I'd been in.

The Touch of the Master's Hand.

Even through this heartache, God is leaving breadcrumbs, little signs to let me know that things will be okay. Despite illness and trials, I am the luckiest.

CHAPTER 29
An Otter in the Universe

The infusion chair feels huge around my small frame. I've lost fifteen pounds now, which is a significant amount considering I was underweight before. Even though I've been sicker than ever, I've started feeling quite hopeful.

Maybe this is simply a stage of grief. Maybe I'm stuck in denial even though it's at the beginning of the list, and I'm already pretty far into this debilitating process. But my mind is so excited for summer. Even though I'm sick, there is so much I want to do: hike, paint, eat out on restaurant patios....

The other day, Mike, the kids, and I painted in our backyard. I had to take frequent breaks, but at the end, excitement bubbled within me, and I felt overjoyed with what we'd done. We each painted a universe complete with planets, stars, and open space. Just seeing how happy the kids were over some spray paint and cheap poster boards, well, that made it all worth it.

Mike had to practically carry me back into the house afterward. I didn't let the kids see how weak I was. We took selfies and smiled broadly. It wasn't until they prepared for bed that Mike helped me put myself back together.

The next day, I held my picture of the universe up and thought, "This puts life in perspective. We're all so minuscule. Even smaller than these specks I painted as stars."

When you start thinking about how massive our world is and how immense the galaxies are, even melanoma doesn't seem like such a big deal. I'm like an ant. An ant with cancer. Pretty sure it's not really *that* big of a deal.

I'm still worried about those court documents I got served a while back. I just don't know what I'd do if I lost my kids. But I finally got an attorney and a court date, and he told me not to worry at all. His dad had cancer, and so he wants to do everything he can to help us get through everything.

"This is inhumane, this paperwork. You don't worry about losing your kids. This man has absolutely no case. You just worry about your health and leave the rest to me."

I thought about all of that again as I sat in the massive infusion chair—about how small I am and how small my problems are when compared to the vastness of all living things. I just need to have peace that it'll all work out.

And when things were truly in perspective, all the fear vanished, and instead, only a calmness remained. I've got this!

We have an attorney who's willing to help even though we have no money.

And I received other big news. In three more weeks, I'll get scans to see if the new therapy is working. Today my blood counts were the best they've been since October. I think we're about to get some good news. There has to be something good going on with all of the other crazy things we've been through lately.

***

When I ran that small-town newspaper, the mayor of Blackfoot told me that if I really wanted to meet some interesting people, I should visit a certain café around eight a.m. on a Friday. So, I did, wearing my most beautiful business dress. It was hilarious to just pull up a chair and sit down by a bunch of men in their eighties and nineties.

"Well, what are you doing?" an especially old man asked. "And who are you?"

"I'm ordering a coffee. What the hell are you doin'?"

They all laughed, and what I didn't know is how much one of those men would change my life.

Fast-forward three years. The Phantom and I have become the best of friends. He's brilliant, well versed, and witty. He took the news hard when he discovered I have cancer.

"But you're so young," he'd said, because although I feel ancient, in his mind, thirty-eight is practically an infant. "Ya know, Elisa. I hate to say it, but I'm losing my spark for life. I guess that's what happens as we age. I'm just getting tired of it all."

My heart felt the immense weight of those words. Even with all my sickness—and profound suffering lately—I still have a spark. It seems that what he faces is even worse than my struggle to survive.

Yesterday, he drove up to my house in a fancy hot rod and visited with my family. "You always talk about playing the violin, but I've never heard you play," he said out of nowhere.

"Do *you* play an instrument?" The question just came to me, and I could hardly believe I'd never asked.

"I play around with the piano, but I'm not very good."

"Well, why don't we jam?"

I grabbed my violin, and he sat at my piano. I didn't know the melody, but it wasn't too hard to pick out. As he played a couple of refrains, I jumped in, and the music just flowed. We crescendoed and quickened at the same times. The music vibrated through both of us as if we were immersed in a rushing river. The moment was truly unforgettable.

When he finished playing that song from the 1940s, I looked at him and smiled. I realized he'd gotten his spark back.

"I could play when I was four," he said. "I just always knew how. It was during the Great Depression, and I'd go play at neighbors' houses for pennies. I'd come home with a whole jar filled with coins. That was a big deal back in those days."

Before leaving, he stepped from his fancy sports car and said, "Hey, Elisa. You've got to get better. When you do, I'll let you drive me around town in my car!"

"Oh, really? Incentive!" I could hardly contain my laughter.

It's amazing how a stranger from three years ago has become such a dear friend. I loved seeing that spark come back into his eyes.

It might have helped set mine ablaze even more.

***

I'm an otter. It's not something I hide. My brother said he's always thought of me as an otter. Imagine my surprise when I found a Native American zodiac and discovered that I actually *am* an otter. I would've picked something different for myself, like a ferocious lion. But that wasn't in the cards.

I had a rough week. I'm in the stage of this sickness where I've started reevaluating things I've already reevaluated. I have a list of shoulda coulda wouldas that stretches to the moon and back. I've worried that maybe I should've read to the kids longer each day or taught them how to play the piano. (Mother's Day always brings this out too.) I should've never gone fake baking at the tanning salon ('cause melanoma). I should've gone to church more... or maybe less. I should've eaten better and been more resolute with many things. And most of all, I should *not* have been such a silly, fun-loving otter.

I cooked with Indy last night. I started talking in a British accent and pretended she was a contestant on my cooking show. I'm still not sure how, but as she showed her culinary prowess, we cut up way too many carrots.

"We better not burn these!" I said, all hoity-toity. "To win or not to win. *That*—my little friend—*is* the question."

She sneaked off after we popped everything in the oven, and I sat at the table, grinning. I could still hear my little girl's giggles as we chopped and mixed. Maybe—just maybe—it's okay that I'm so silly. There's a time and place for everything and a need for all kinds of people in this world, right? And just when I was finally coming to terms with who I am, I got a message from Ruby.

> *I got a tattoo today!*
> *What?*
> *Now I have you tattooed on me!*

And then—the same gorgeous kid who shaved her head when I lost my hair, that same sparkling light who's been there every second since I got cancer—sent me a picture. On her arm, right in plain sight, is a beautiful otter.

Sometimes it takes the acceptance of the people we love most for us to see the beauty and value in ourselves. I was getting there on my own, but it sure felt nice for my oldest daughter to simply love me for me—the same way I love her for exactly who she is. I'm so proud of that kid. She gives me courage to let go of the past. I've done the best I can, and that has to be good enough.

***

I once read a book, *StrengthsFinder*, that claimed it could help you find your greatest strengths. The magnitude of finding the greatest strengths idea wasn't a new concept but boasting that it could actually help me discover mine was. I eagerly read the premise, thinking strengths are things like courage and intellect. Tom Rath wrote that focusing on strengths is much more important than honing weaknesses—that we can go much further in life if we develop our God-given talents rather than trying to eliminate flaws.

When it came time for me to discover my strengths, I can't tell you how excited I was. The StrengthsFinder test was much more like an employer's personality test than I had guessed.

My greatest strength wasn't something awesome like longevity or harmony. It was positivity.

I stared at the screen in shock. How could positivity be a strength? I'd begun to think of strengths as someone's superpower, but how could that be mine? You'd never see a superhero named Captain Positivity. Why couldn't mine be something like courage? I turned off the computer a bit bummed. Positivity? Seriously?

I've never forgotten the results of that test. And even as I've been having a hard time lately, instead of dwelling on my flaws, I've tried to remember my greatest strength. The ironic thing is that there is some power to it—for me. I could be trapped in a hard situation, feeling there's no way out, but there's something to be said for being positive. It takes a horrible experience and flips it on its head. Positivity throws a window into a doorless room.

A friend called yesterday and said she's so sorry for all I'm going through. I told her, "It's in the dark times when we can try to make our light shine brighter."

She gasped at the end of the conversation. "It's crazy. But I think you're lucky you have cancer."

I accidentally let out a laugh. "I wouldn't wish this on *anyone*. But I have to see the bright side."

So, while it's not the fantastic superpower I'd hoped for, it's helping me through some pretty dark times. Maybe the strength I have isn't as bad as I once thought. I'm learning so much about myself. It's sad that it took something like this, but I'm proud to be coming to a deeper understanding of who I am.

CHAPTER 30
Omnipotent

I should've never announced that I don't believe Jesus is the son of God. I write for a newspaper in Island Park, Idaho—and I even wrote a column about it last month. That was like saying, "Hey, I'm the weak one in the herd! Come after me!"

I mean, I knew I'd get backlash, but the hundreds of religious messages I received blew me away. I got correspondence from people of religions I'd never even heard of. People said to find God I should go to a mosque, become a Jehovah's Witness, join the LDS church, ask Jesus to be my Lord and Savior, meditate three times a day, find a spirit guide, go on a root cleanse, and find spirits of higher vibrations. The list goes on and on. What they all forgot to consider is that maybe I've already found God.

In fact, I think I've felt Him since I had a prayer box as a little girl. And then, when I learned to play the violin, I felt Him even more. As if a musical string connected me directly to God, I could feel His love pouring in me and through me as I played, just like I knew *He* could feel my love going right back to Him.

But according to some of these people, if I'd just done what they'd said—if I just had more faith—I'd already be healed.

I felt like I'd been sitting on a peaceful beach and these messages were deadly waves crashing against me. I even had someone send strangers to my house to convert me. I spent thirty minutes trying to tell them "no" when I'd just finished work, my kids were in school, and I should've been resting.

Instead of converting me, these people have helped me have an even stronger faith in God's love. He doesn't need to be tied to stupid manmade rules. He found me despite what all these people believe.

Even after my son died—even *then*—God still stayed by my side. He gave me the fortitude to get through that. I feel like I'll be all right.

I don't know what the future holds, but I figure an omnipotent God sure does. If He saw fit to create me, then I trust Him to judge me too—after all, He's God.

For now, I'll continue envisioning myself in the hand of God. That's the place I find solace when I'm having hard days. I could be wrong about this, just like everyone else could be wrong, but at least I've found some comfort in putting my faith in God and playing my violin for Him.

***

The MRI machine whirred around me once again, this time to take pictures of my brain. When I saw the radiation oncologist about this previously, the cancerous tumor in my brain had gotten smaller, but the cancer wasn't dying like we'd hoped.

I worried about all of this as the machine tha-whumped and buzzed. Nausea overcame me for a minute, which I'd worried about. For two months, I've thrown up nearly every day. I've understood mental suffering, but I've never understood what physical suffering was truly like until now. I imagined the horror of throwing up with my mask on—in the MRI machine.

The music in the room grew louder. And the words—about when the water finally cleanses you—surprisingly settled everything inside of me. I listened to the '60s singer and imagined those cleansing waters. What would that feel like to take a swim and be totally cleansed? One of the bizarre things on my bucket list is to go skinny dipping. I wondered if I'd ever be brave enough to go.

After the techs removed my IV and slid me from the machine, my mother-in-law and I went to the cafeteria.

We quickly ate and ended up pulling out a deck of cards. "Rummy?" I asked, and she nodded.

It quickly became apparent that since our last trip to the hospital, my mother-in-law has become quite a card shark. I desperately wished for a wild card. *Why doesn't regular rummy have wilds?* I could just pull that one special card from the deck and finally have a chance of winning!

I looked up wild cards the other day. It meant a lot more than I realized. It can also be someone who is picked to win a contest because of something extraordinary.

I so wish God would pick me to be a wildcard. I don't need to draw one. I need to *be* a wildcard.

We went to my appointment after that to review the results of the MRI. First, the nurse practitioner came in and helped us. Then a random doctor I'd never seen, a radiologist, came in. He reviewed the scans over and over. He was very cryptic as he continued zooming in on the scans.

"I think it's showing some improvement. I'll go get your regular doctor."

As my mother-in-law and I waited, I nervously kicked my legs just a little bit. It's so hard being patient, waiting for scans to be taken, then waiting to hear good or bad news.

My regular radiation oncologist finally came in, reviewed the scans, sat back, and viewed the scans again. My mind wandered. Why had the first doctor left the room like that? Maybe it was bad news. I grew so scared.

"Do you see the second tumor?" I asked. "The one that isn't cancer?"

"I don't see a second tumor at all. And it wouldn't have just disappeared. That means you've never had a second tumor."

But multiple doctors had told me there was a second tumor.

"In fact, I don't...." She paused.

"What do you see?" I asked after a moment.

"Well, here's your brain from November." She pointed little things out that are specific to me. "And here's your brain today. There's no cancer, Elisa. Your brain... is cancer free."

She said some other things about how I still have cancer in my back, neck, and hip. But I really wasn't listening anymore.

"But tumors in the brain can be stubborn—especially melanoma," she said. "This is really, really good news."

I couldn't help it. I stood up and hugged my mother-in-law. She beamed at the news. Then I turned to the doctor—and I hugged her too (mask and all)!

"You know how you asked me to fill out that paperwork for your court case?" she asked. "About keeping your kids?"

I nodded, holding my breath.

"I'll have it ready for you by tomorrow. This new development should help you quite a bit. You can call and get it from the nurse. You're not out of the woods yet, but this news is pretty tremendous."

"Oh! Thank you! Thank you so very much!"

My hand shook. No one could have fully understood what all of this meant. My kids are my world. So much more than my health has been on the line.

My appointment ended, and I went and told all the nurses right outside of the room. Then, at the front desk, I told all the receptionists! I ended up telling several other strangers on the way out of the hospital. The whole time, my mother-in-law smiled and shook her head. I just wanted to shout from the rooftops: "My brain is cancer free!"

I still don't know how or why it happened, but I'm so grateful to everyone who prayed for me. And I'm so grateful to God.

Like the doctor said, I still have such a long journey ahead of me. The immunotherapy is hard on my body, but the fact that both radiation and immunotherapy have helped eradicate the cancer from my brain gives me hope it can work in the rest of my body.

I've had so many doctors tell me I only had two years to live from. But yesterday, two doctors gave me a completely different prognosis. They gave me my faith back.

I can't believe how fortunate I am. I don't know what the future holds, but I do know it holds a longer life than I previously anticipated. I got home and told my family. Indy cried and hugged me. The joy in all their faces was worth more to me than anything. This does feel like a miracle—I think it kind of is. Maybe God did pick me to be a wildcard after all.

***

I bring my kids to church every Sunday that I can—even though I'm still definitely not religious. But today went differently; I got so sick I couldn't stay. I told Indy we'd use a trick my mom taught me. Wait for the next prayer, then exit discreetly. One problem remained: Trey sat somewhere else with his friend.

So, we waited, but ruining expectations, they didn't pray *forever*. I gathered my stuff and tried to hold my keys like brass knuckles so they wouldn't jangle.

"Bow your heads while we pray," they finally said.

"Now!" I whispered to Indy like we were a SWAT team. "Go. Go! Go!" After almost tripping on someone's purse handle, we made it to where Trey sat, and I just knew the deacon would soon wrap up the world's shortest prayer. Everyone would see me trying to get my son to leave. It would be the most awkward thing ever, especially since the church was completely full.

"Trey," I whispered, but the kid was intently praying—for once. "Trey! TREY!"

Then he turned with his eyes still closed and shushed me. "They're praying."

"And I'm sick."

He opened his eyes. "Oh! Sorry, Mom."

"In Jesus name," the deacon's voice slowed just as we opened the back door to freedom. "Amen."

If I hadn't been so sick, I would've felt like Indiana Jones leaving that cave in his first movie. Because it *was* sort of awesome! We left church early and got away with it. Sometimes being an adult does have its perks.

After we got home, I immediately went to bed. Before I could fall asleep, I heard my kids talking. "That's the first time I've actually wanted to be in church."

"Yeah, me too," Indy said. "I was really excited to hear the sermon."

"Yeah!" Trey said emphatically.

I can't win, but there are some days when we have to think about ourselves. Plus, I've never puked in a church — because that's God's house. Disaster averted!

I'll try again next Sunday. Better luck next time? Plus, it is kind of fun imagining people's faces when they realized we'd just vanished during the prayer.

After the docs told me my brain tumors are gone, I've decided some miraculous things can happen when we pray.

CHAPTER 31
Melanoma Fashion Model

I stand by the comment, "Give me a bed and a bucket, and I'm good." But things have gotten harder. And even though a friend warned me, I had no concept of how tough immunotherapy would be. It sounds a lot nicer than chemotherapy, but unfortunately, it's not. It's like calling a fart a unicorn.

Strange to think that the tumors in my brain are gone, yet I'm sicker than I've been this whole time with nausea, weakness, and fatigue. They doubled my doses and the frequency of the immunotherapy, so no wonder. On the flip side, this is what might help me beat this thing.

I had a fever all night and dreamed that Mike and I were floating in a freezing ocean where all we had was each other and the occasional flip of a nefarious tail. I called in sick to work, which totally sucks! Before this cancer business, I hadn't called in sick since 2014.

Then, I slept most of the day, unable to do much else.

After I woke up, I tried to find someone else online who's been through exactly the same situation. It took a while, but I found a man from 2018 who had melanoma tumors in his brain that went away after numerous immunotherapy treatments. But he had some other stubborn tumors that wouldn't leave—and they just happen to be in the same places as mine (spine, neck, etc.).

So, I saw that in 2018 he responded to a thread about melanoma, saying how terrible the side effects of immunotherapy were. He got massive rashes everywhere that itched like crazy. He couldn't hold anything down, until he only weighed 120 pounds. The doctors eventually made him take breaks on his treatments for fear that he'd lose too much—and there was a comment saying how the side effects from immunotherapy almost killed him.

I read this entire story with complete interest—until it just stopped. I had no idea if the man lived or died. What a terrible feeling to not know.

I had his name and his wife's name too, so I looked them up on Facebook. To my dismay, his wife had been put in an assisted living home in 2019. And the man himself, well, the trail went cold, and I worried that he hadn't made it after all.

It might sound crazy, but I started scrolling through his stories, wanting to know more about this man who suffered from the same thing as me. It was odd because he's also a writer. And I just couldn't shake the feeling that I understood this person because of everything we've both gone through. I saw a book giveaway he'd held, some posts about cancer, and other things.

After a while, I decided to send him a message. It wasn't a very hopeful message. And I waited most of the evening, to no avail.

Early the next day I grabbed yet another bottle of water. Lately, the main thing I can keep down is clear liquid, which is tragic because I could really go for a hot dog with green peppers and onions right now.

More time passed, and I started to lose hope not only for this man but for myself. This type of suffering, it's just hard to put into words. And just when I had completely given up, my phone binged.

Yes, I am still here.

He'd actually responded.

I know these stories might sound silly, but when something as small as this propels us through each day, it's actually quite big.

It was fun to talk with him. Like so many other people I've spoken with, he is inspiring. And you know what, I just might buy one of his books.

***

When I stepped into the hospital elevator, the poor couple with me looked grim.

"How are you?" the elderly man asked in a monotone.

"The sun is shining! It's a beautiful day." Forget that I'd just discovered that my liver is failing. The doctor told me to hang out by infusions because I'd need to be admitted as soon as they got me a hospital bed. "I'm just fighting the good fight, staying strong, trying to beat cancer. 'Cause what else did I have to do with my time? Nothing! I'd get bored if I wasn't so damn busy trying to stay strong. Am I right?"

The couple just stared at me like a genuine lunatic had joined them in that tiny, locked, moving box.

Bing! The doors opened.

"That's my stop." I waved and got off, positive that I'd just scared the crap out of the poor, sad couple.

Just before the elevator door closed, the woman stuck her hand out and stepped into the hallway. "Miss?"

"Yeah," I said.

"We, well, we really like your positive attitude. Don't lose it. If you lose it, it's hard to find again."

I nodded. "I hope the two of you will have the most wonderful day. I have a feeling I'll be thinking about you—and sending you good vibes—for most of it!"

She went back into the elevator, and I headed off, hoping that whatever situation they're in, it'll somehow get better.

I also hope I'll never lose my optimism. Some days are hard. I've cried out of fear, pain, or just grief because of my altered health. But that's the thing I've realized about joy. It's not like happiness. Happiness comes and goes. Joy stays. It's a way of being. When people persevere, they see a wall and keep trying to knock it down, get over it, overcome it even when they know they will fail. Having joy is the same. I *choose* to be joyful despite hardship and even failure. Always, I must choose joy.

So, what am I doing today? I'm fighting the good fight, waiting for a hospital bed, trying to kick cancer's butt. Like I said before, what was I gonna do with my time anyway?

***

During my stay in the hospital, doctors discovered the cancer treatments had been what started hurting my liver. I guessed they're just working a little too well, putting my cells into overdrive.

My fingers tapped the food tray, and the lukewarm coffee rippled in response. They let us order off a fancy menu for each meal, but unfortunately, I'd been put on a liquid diet: coffee, water, juice, Jell-O, and broth.

"So, I won't get out today?" I asked the doctor.

"No, Elisa. We need to get this under control. Your liver numbers are off the charts. You're lucky we caught it now, so your liver will still have a chance to heal."

I'd seen my lab numbers. I was in stage three liver failure (with stage four being the worst).

"Wait! I really wanted to get out today because it's my son's birthday," I implored him. "He's turning thirteen. I didn't expect to be here for days. I'm supposed to teach him and his friends how to spray paint the universe on poster boards. He was so excited. And so was I."

"I'm sorry. I really am. I know that this must be hard, but we just can't let you leave until the steroids start bringing these numbers down. It's not safe."

I nodded, and the guy simply walked out of the room and shut the door behind him.

I pushed the food tray to the side of my bed and stared at the thin sheet covering my legs. I hadn't turned on the TV at all since I got there. Instead, I'd been reading books a clergy representative brought me from the hospital's library. *To Life!* I read the title of a Jewish book and set it aside. I'd selected my religion as Jewish on the intake paperwork, just so I could meet some different clergy members. Maybe I'd read that book later, but right now I needed to figure out Trey's birthday.

I picked up my cellphone. "Mike," I said. "How's it going?"

"I took the day off. And just in case you can't come home, I've got the whole thing figured out. Your friend

Katy's coming to help with Trey's party. I've been watching painting shows on YouTube all day. I'll teach the boys how to paint—I know it won't be you, but I'll do the best I can. I'm even making a cake!"

"You're amazing. It'll be perfect. I just wish I could be there."

"I know you do. And Trey knows too. Don't feel bad. You can take him to do something fun—anything—as soon as you're feeling better and you're out of there."

"Okay," I said. "You'll have Trey call me tonight?"

"Absolutely," Mike said.

That afternoon, Mike did everything he promised. Indy helped with the party, along with some of my friends. Trey called and gushed about his painting and how Mike was letting every single one of the boys stay the night. "It'll be epic! We're even ordering pizza!"

I couldn't help laughing into the phone.

"We'll do something fun when you get back?" he asked. "Just me and you?"

"Just me and you," I said.

"Maybe we can paint something again. I'm not gonna lie—I'm getting pretty good!"

Mike got on the phone after that because Trey's friends were calling him. "So, what are you up to tonight, sweetheart?"

"I might order some more Jell-O." I laughed. "Strawberry this time. Seriously though. I feel so much better knowing Trey's having a great time. Thank you for everything. And don't worry about me—they're getting my numbers down. You know I always make the best of things." I heard the nurse coming shortly after that and panicked. "I've got to go," I said. "Love you."

"Love you!" he said and hung up the phone.

The nurses are constantly coming into the room to take my vitals, draw my blood, or knock me out with medicine. I just needed a break. So, I rushed into the bathroom and when someone knocked on the door I hollered, "Give me a little bit, please. Thank you so much!"

After her footsteps faded, I investigated the hospital mirror. No wonder they wouldn't let me out— I looked like Medusa. Thank God Mike couldn't see me like this. I could just imagine him looking at me and turning to stone. We *both* didn't need to die from cancer-related complications!

I patted my hair down with wet paper towels, grabbed my push-up bra from my hospital bag, and decided to have a fashion shoot in the bathroom. The nurses would've killed me if they knew, and each time someone came in, I told them I was pooping.

If I tucked and tied the gown just right, it did look kind of sexy. I made it into a sleeveless number and stuffed the fabric right into my boobs—then made sure it framed my butt!

It took a moment to get all the finishing touches, and after about ten minutes I had cleavage up to my neck and a gown fit for the psych unit. I limped around, then would turn and point into the mirror before blowing a kiss.

I took a bunch of pictures in the mirror after that and even posted a couple to Facebook. Some of the responses made me break out laughing. "You really make the best of the moment." "That's right, don't let cancer get you down." "That hospital gown looks HAWT," a hilarious barista wrote.

I decided to take my show on the road. Well, not really on the road, but out of the bathroom anyway because the toilet was cramping my style. Hopefully, the nurse wouldn't be in for a minute, and I could get some hilarious photos by my room's window. So, I hobbled across the room and quickly sprawled across the seating area under the bay window. "Draw me like one of your French girls, Jack." The line from *Titanic* made me giggle as I donned pouty lips and prepared to take the silliest photo ever. Mike would think this was hilarious!

The door opened. Ever. So. Slowly.

I stayed frozen in embarrassment as my frumpy Broom Hilda nurse stared at me, gaping. Unfortunately, she did not appreciate seeing my $5,000 cleavage. "What in heaven's name?" she finally said.

"I'm trying to make the best of the moment," I said. Then I winked at someone who has *no* sense of humor.

"I've come to get your vitals but forget it. I'll be back later."

Then she slipped away, and I laughed so hard.

I waited there for a while, surprised to be smiling despite the circumstances. So, I couldn't be there for Trey's birthday, but he'd had an amazing time, and we would do something fun later.

I could hardly wait to get out of here. Mike sent me a picture of Trey's painting from his party; he really is getting quite good!

***

They discharged me from the hospital and Ruby helped bring me home. We quickly found our truck.

"Time to go back to Idaho," I squealed.

But the driver's door completely deflated my hopes when it wouldn't shut.

"What the...?" Ruby faltered.

"Maybe try lifting it and slamming it?" I asked, thinking it'd gotten off kilter.

So, she did, sending a sound bellowing through the parking garage. But we couldn't get the door to close. After using my cell's flashlight, further inspection showed that the metal latch had busted, wedging inside so far that the door remained permanently ajar.

We nearly tore up our hands trying to get the piece out. "If we can move the damn thing, then I can strap the door closed so we can get back to Idaho."

"How can we drive like this? The door will flap in the wind."

"I'll drive. And we'll tighten 'er down," I said. Sure, I was still sick—and some things felt like were too much on top of everything, but I didn't want to show my daughter that a door could best me. "You just keep me company."

I could've cried. I felt so damn tired bending and trying to get the latch out, striving once again to be strong. Finally, we slammed the door and got it closed enough—after shoving ourselves up against the cold metal—that I could slip a strap through the driver's and passenger's windows. It would be a windy ride home with a door that couldn't close all the way, but at least we could finally leave the cancer hospital.

It was at this point that a sniveling, bald man broached us. Pointy nose prominent and beady eyes judging, he seemed personally offended.

"Wanna try slamming that door a little harder next time? You could make even more noise!" He stopped to breathe deeply, obviously mad from far more than this moment in the parking garage. "You're causing quite a scene."

I knew he had cancer too. But he has something much worse—a mean attitude. Normally I'd feel bad for him, reach out, and turn the other cheek. But then I thought how instead of asking how we were, or offering to help, he'd simply come over to make things worse.

"Sorry. We're just desperate to get back to—"

"Slamming your door!"

"Ya know," I said, and a bit of moxie filled my voice, "maybe I will slam it—just *one* more time."

But, of course, I didn't. After I got in the passenger side and shimmied behind the steering wheel, I backed up and waved to the gape-jawed man who'd only offered to give us cynicism.

"What is wrong with some people?" Ruby asked from the passenger seat. "He seriously came over just to be rude?" And it did seem counterproductive that he'd walked all the way over to us—when he obviously wasn't feeling well in the first place—just because he'd been angry.

"He must have too much on his plate. I guess he can handle his problems his way, and we can handle ours another. That's all *we* can control right now."

We ended up having the most wonderful conversation on the way home. It didn't matter that our A/C didn't work, the truck was missing chunks from the seats, or that the door was jerry-rigged shut.

"It's off to Idaho," I practically bellowed, so happy to be free. Even as the wind styled my hair like the '80s, both Ruby and I smiled almost the whole way home.

CHAPTER 32
Stop Dying and Start Living

That moment when....

You bring your boy fishin' for his "after birthday" celebration. You might rent the world's crappiest motel room, eat take-out pizza, and stay up late playing cards and watching *River Monsters*, but it's better than anything in the whole damn world.

The next morning he'll probably wake up before the sun, excited to revisit a spot he discovered the day before.

As time passes, you'll scout out different spots, even share tricks of the fishin' trade. "You like *that*?" or "You do *this*?" he'll ask as you show him a new way to bait hooks.

Then, as you sit on a bank and trace a stick in the mud, he switches gears, and tells you how much he looks up to you.

"You know," you say, "you're kind like your grandfather and good like your stepdad. You're the best of everyone, all mixed up together."

This makes him so happy he busts with laughter; it's almost too much joy for a thirteen-year-old to handle. "You think so?"

You nod.

"Thanks, Mom. But I hope I'm just a *little* like you too."

"Just a little?" You throw a worm at him, and as it accordions past his face, you both guffaw over how hilarious it looked.

After hours, there's finally a fish on your line, but not his. That just won't do! So, you think of something quick. "Hey, we should head out. But my back hurts awfully bad. Can you reel in my line? Too bad we didn't catch a thing."

He takes care of his first before gingerly picking up your pole. That's when his eyes light up like a GloFish.

"You got one." He's so surprised he's almost shaking. "You got one! Oh, Mom! You did it. I think it's a big one too."

"He's all yours."

Your son beams, so damn happy. And as he hauls in that trout, you would've thought the kid just harpooned a whale. Even if you're covered in mud, and worm guts line your fingernails, you're awfully happy, living in the moment. With fishing, maybe that's just part of the jig.

After a little while longer, the two of you stay alone by the motionless water. You don't care what size of trout you caught, the age of the hook you used, or even if you wasted your money on garlic PowerBait. You made another memory.

I didn't get to celebrate Trey's actual birthday with him, but I think we both got something better. My son really does make every day the best day ever.

***

When we chance losing what really matters, things get clear. The loss of a loved one, a dream, an ability can magnify our "truth."

Lately, I've watched my family sacrifice to trade time — possibly the most valuable construct we have.

"If you want to move to another state, don't put it off for me," I said to our daughter.

"But I don't want to miss time with you. This whole thing has put everything in perspective."

These words mean more than anyone can fathom, but as the person who's sick, I don't want people sacrificing dreams for me.

Mike did this. At the age of nineteen, he'd planned a move to Seattle. Almost more than anything, he wanted to leave Utah and get his pilot's license. But life took a turn.

His dad got cancer, and Mike refused to leave. He traded an ideal for something invaluable: memories with his dad.

It's crazy how priorities change when weighed against the threat of death.

Time passed. Mike's dad recovered, and he's been doing awesome since. But Mike never moved to Seattle. He landed a job at a food-processing plant like his father and grandfather before him, bought a house, and married a single mom, who then got cancer. It seems fate has brought him right back where he started.

"I've watched him give up so much to take care of me," I told a dear friend. "He's worked, tended to the kids, waited on me after surgeries and treatments. You should've seen what he did for Trey's birthday!"

"That's what you do when you love someone."

I sighed. "It's so strange how life turns out though, right? Can you believe he wanted to be a pilot?" I briefly relayed the story. "I wish Mike could actually fly a plane someday. We must all have dreams, locked up deep inside. He's just done so much for me. I wish I could give him the world."

The next day I lazily opened my computer to find a message from my friend. She'd set up a time for Mike to visit a local airport.

"What?" I balked at the screen.

It's all taken care of.

Mike would get an official lesson where he'd actually fly an airplane!

I would love to come and be there when you do this, if you'd be okay with it.

I could hardly wait to see her, and I couldn't believe she'd done something so wonderful.

This isn't about feeling bad, about regrets or lost opportunities. We all age. We all have responsibilities. But this is a reminder that life is meant to be lived.

Last weekend held one of the best days of my life: to see Mike step out of a plane he'd just landed. He glowed, excited about the wind and the speed. His arms moved with such animation, swooping and diving as he weaved his story.

My dear friend's smile is etched on my heart forever.

"I just love you," I told her.

"You too, Elisa." Then she beamed, watching Mike bounce around like Tigger, telling us how grateful he felt for the opportunity.

Goodness multiplied seems like a perpetual-motion machine that can cast out any type of regret or fear. I felt such a sense of wonder seeing Mike reveling in the moment, and I'm beyond grateful to my generous friend and her husband who made this possible. They gave us something unforgettable: time well spent with those we love.

***

Who knew that having cancer could bring so many people together? But I've written all about it, been open and honest about my fears, doubts, and even peace with it all. And what's happened in return has been amazing.

I've met people who have survived cancer or are still battling it. They've felt the same as me and now have someone new to talk with. I've seen people miraculously healed from tumors. I've met people who later died, and now I know their surviving family members. I even wrote about my doubts with religion and was discovered that I wasn't the only person who had experienced an exorcism as a teenager. That same assistant pastor did exorcisms on two other kids I knew. Each of us had no idea about the other experiences. After over twenty years of feeling like a bad person, absolution came with the knowledge that I wasn't alone. That's what cancer has taught me. I've never really been alone, even when I thought I was. Family and friends have been here. God was always here, too.

I've had some very good news and some hard news recently. My brain remains free of cancer, which is a miracle in and of itself. The doctor told me brain tumors are usually the last to go, if at all. But since my liver started failing a few weeks ago, we had to stop cancer treatments for a moment so my liver can recover. This really *is* a battle. And just when I think I'm starting to win, there might be a sobering setback that momentarily buckles my knees. Like that stupid court paperwork or a deferment of treatments.

There's been no more news on the court stuff except that I got my doctor's note and gave it to my attorney. He said it's the solid key to winning our case. "No one should try taking someone's children because the parent has cancer, especially when they're the parent who's been the main one involved for years," he said on our most recent phone call. "You and your kids need to be together. Their love is probably what's helping keep you strong so you can get better."

I keep thinking about how his dad died from cancer. I think that experience made him extra empathetic to clients who struggled through these same issues.

What I wanted to say isn't how tough this is, but rather how beautiful it's been to see the love and support from so many people. Laying everything bare, although terrifying, is liberating. I thought people might shun me for some of the things I've blatantly shared, but instead, people have selflessly shown love, and just accepted me despite how scared I've been about suffering or even death.

None of us know what the future holds or if we'll get to experience a tomorrow. That uncertainty can be terrifying. But when we have the love and support of each other, life is so much easier. It's beautiful. I have more flaws than most. People have accepted me regardless, one of the greatest gifts of my life. I've been so fortunate to see it while I'm still alive. I think everyone has this support, they just don't always get to witness it.

I'll have more scans this week and my biweekly labs. We'll find out where to go from here and if they'll continue a lighter version of immunotherapy, or if they'll start chemo.

Things are really starting to look better, but this is still war. War isn't meant to be easy.

I pray that God will continue to refine me. I better buckle up though. Apparently, trying to be the best version of myself is gonna take a *lot* more time!

***

"There are just so many things I never got to do," I confessed to Mike. "Some things are really dumb, and others seem big, like going to Italy."

He pursed his lips, making his bushy mustache and beard seem even fuller than normal. "I'm so sorry, sweetheart."

We've talked a lot lately about both of our hopes and dreams. It's interesting to see what things don't seem as important and what things still do.

That night he stayed up late, saying he wanted to plan a surprise and that it would arrive in two weeks. "You're still doing that book signing at the end of the month?" he asked.

I nodded. A charter school in Blackfoot had asked me to be part of a special carnival where I would speak to kids about my YA fantasy novel and encourage them to love both reading and writing. The grades would range all the way from kindergarten to twelfth grade, and I'd made a presentation I hoped kids of all ages would love.

"I just need to really rest up before then. It'll be awesome, but I know it'll take a lot out of me. I'll be speaking to the kids for about an hour." I rolled over and propped myself on my elbow. "Why do you ask?"

"No reason. Oh, and what size does Indy wear now?"

"Women's small." I raised a brow. Mike makes life an adventure.

Two weeks later, Mike called Indy and me into the kitchen. "Okay, Indy. You know your mom's book, *The Sword of Senack*?"

"Yeah."

"Well, she's having a big book signing where she'll be talking to hundreds of kids in Blackfoot. And she needs your help."

I started to smile. What in the world was he doing?

"I bought your mom a full outfit so she can dress up like one of the characters. It's actually on her bucket list. And I bought you one too."

Indy and I stared at one another, our eyes growing wide with wonder as Mike furnished two wigs (bright aqua and purple), two flowing dresses, oceanic jewelry, and sparkly makeup. Finally, after all of these years, I could dress up as a genuine Thenian!

"So, your mom will do a signing dressed in character. Can you help her by doing the same?"

"Yes! Yes—yes! I get to wear a wig?"

"Absolutely," Mike said.

She jumped up in the air and hugged both of us, even though I hadn't done anything. "*This* is the coolest day ever!"

On the day of the signing, we had a blast getting ready and doing each other's makeup. Indy's skin sparkled like a real mermaid, and her fake eyelashes made her look reminiscent of a cartoon. We appraised one another in the mirror.

"This is pretty neat," Indy said. "I've always wanted to look like Aliya from your book."

Trey offered to help with the signing as well, but in a different way. He carried tons of boxes and didn't even complain. As he and Mike set everything up, I thought about what good kids we have. I wasn't sure if we'd gotten closer because of the experience with cancer, but I had noticed a tremendous change in everyone. We're finally rallying as a family.

The presentation went flawlessly. I don't know how, but I think I did inspire the charter school children because so many of them stayed to talk afterward. I'd been able to read an excerpt from my book. The room hushed as I impersonated a witch's voice. A fan had blown my direction in that moment, and my hair enchantingly drifted past my face. "Come with me," I crooned the words, then looked at the children. "Come with me *into* the ocean."

I got chills at this point, because it just felt like pure, unadulterated magic scented the air.

I read about "Indy," the actual name of the character in *The Sword of Senack*, and how she'd followed an evil witch into the ocean. "Her legs went into the water, then her waist." I almost whispered. "Her neck." A high school student scooted forward in his seat, hanging onto each word. "And then her head went ever so gently... into the water."

I glanced over at Indy. She perched behind me so the kids would have a great visual as I read the story.

"After my sister disappeared under the ashen waves, the green-eyed witch turned to me." My voice cracked with the coldness this part would require. "I'll be back for you." I pointed to all the children and put my book down. "*All...* of you!"

Everyone stayed quiet, but then a tiny kindergartner started clapping, before a rainstorm of applause followed.

At the end of the presentation, I played my violin as an accompaniment to a silly story volunteers helped me write in front of the live audience. And just before we left for the night, I gave away some copies of my book: one to a junior high student who "can't afford many books" and cried over the copy, and one to a darling little boy. He lives in our neighborhood and practically floated when he found out his neighbor "actually wrote a book about dragons!"

Indy and Trey visited with different kids about what it's like having a mom who's an author, and my heart filled to the brim with contentment. Mike sat down at one point, wearing the wig he'd just borrowed from Indy, and I erupted with laughter. He'd made the night a success.

The next day, I'd just hung up the aqua wig in my closet when someone knocked on my front door.

"Um, hi?" I said.

A little boy stood on my porch with his grandma. He held a colorfully wrapped package and a smile that could've won over any politician.

"You're the kid from last night," I said, beaming at the boy. He was the happy guy I'd given a copy of my book to.

"Come in, come in," I said, not even wondering what they were doing. That's one of the remarkable things about living in a small town.

"I stayed up and read a lot of your book," he admitted.

"You did?"

"He couldn't put it down," his grandma said as she settled onto the small couch in my front room. "Then he asked if we could go get you something special from the store."

He handed me the package. "I remembered this when I read your book. It's Constance — the bad guy in your book."

I slowly unwrapped the package and could hardly believe what they'd given me: a beautiful statue of a figure that actually looked just like the villain in my book!

"This is the sweetest, most wonderful—"

"Can I get a picture with you?" he asked. "I just really, really like the book."

"Sure!"

"Can you... put the wig on?"

I grinned. "Give me a second."

As fast as I could, I threw on the dress and the wig. You should've seen the little guy's face when I came back into the room. His grandma took a picture of us together, holding the figurine. I knew I'd never forget that moment, ever.

After they left, I wondered about the events of the last two days. I'd checked something off my bucket list, and now I'd always have a fun outfit and a figurine to remember just how wonderful the experience had been. I was so grateful for everything, and to still be making memories.

***

We recently received something quite disturbing in the mail. Someone anonymously sent us a document detailing how certain people are chosen to be the bride of Christ while others are not. These others are "people marked, stricken down with sicknesses and trials, so others will know those who are *not* God's chosen people." It went on to say that—if I've been wondering—this is why I'm sick. I haven't been "chosen."

This upset Mike, and he didn't want to tell me about the document for a few days. When he finally did, because I knew something was eating him alive, the news made my stomach roll.

I prayed, "Dear God, I'd really like to spend eternity with you. I can't imagine existing away from you. So, if you have room for me in heaven, that would be great." I paused. "Why would someone want to hurt me so badly when I'm already going through so much? Why would a 'Christian' send this to me?" I exhaled slowly. "Anyway, thanks for listening. Amen."

It took a couple of days, but after the shock wore off, the whole thing reminded me of something I've finally realized about sickness, trials, and flaws. Let me back up though so I can explain this fully. When I first got cancer, I coped by painting.

I've been working my whole life to be worth something, to produce things that made me feel of value—start businesses, author books, play various instruments—to be refined and rid myself of flaws. But when you get a cancer diagnosis, especially stage four, that is not a sign of perfection.

My dad told me the other day about how God sent him perfect children. I teared up a little, thinking about how I'm not perfect and cancer is just another blaring sign of that, a beacon saying, "I'm defective—and I'm definitely not good enough."

But then I remembered my paintings. They are so terrible that I could never make money from them. My first few paintings were extra horrendous because I'd go back and try to fix the flaws over and over. But spray paint, my cheap medium of choice, dries so quickly that things stay permanent and too much paint just turns to brown soup.

Now, after months of this, I've learned to work around the flaws. In fact, some of my favorite parts of these pictures are things that went wrong, the unfixable turned perfect. And in these flaws, I'm seeing such incredible beauty, and the paintings are improving too.

A misplaced white dot turned to snowcapped mountains. A buck transformed into a majestic antelope. Even a boulder turned into the silhouette of a bear.

As I painted yesterday, it hit me again. Who cares if everyone knows I'm flawed, sick, and experiencing trials? That doesn't designate me as someone shunned by God. This is simply an opportunity to become stronger and rise to the occasion. Maybe this is my chance to shine despite hardship. Just like these paintings, I'll use the undesirable to my advantage. Although I'm exhausted and battling for my life, my soul is becoming resilient. And even things like this judgmental document are making me a better person. It's a mixture of refinement and acceptance; there must be a balance.

Every day, I embrace the imperfections and find beauty in them no matter how hard that might be. It's a great mindset to live by. Whether I get better or not, I will let positivity buoy me forward.

***

At some point you stop dying and start living.

I thought this as I sat at the edge of a beautiful river. Mike and I went on a date, and I decided to be done dying.

I went from fully clothed to shucking nearly everything in a matter of seconds. As I floated out in the frigid water, Mike's eyes quadrupled in size.

"Well, you sure ain't boring."

I snorted, so happy—and cold. "Come on in. The water's ffffiiiine."

But he didn't want to come in. And then my legs cramped up on me.

Cancer makes you want to do things you previously lacked the courage for, but now it's almost too late.

"Oh, my gosh, Mike," I said. "My legs are freezing up."

"Sure. Sure."

"No, really." And the current started to take me. I could just imagine myself floating straight to some farmer's crop, where they'd make me walk out—in all my glory.

Mike, that good ol' Eagle Scout, didn't want to get his pants and shoes wet, so he stripped down to his skivvies, taking forever like some show in Vegas. When I thought he'd finally save me, that man freaked out because of mud and took so long I thought we'd missed the second coming of Christ. Anyway, Mike eventually dipped one dainty foot in and snatched me from a future with a successful farmer.

We held each other, both of us covered in mud. Then we put our clothes back on.

I swear we haven't laughed that hard in a long time. I leaned back on a rock, resting in the arms of my own personal hero, and grinned.

I've grown to love my life too much through all of this—appreciating every single moment.

CHAPTER 33
Fiddle for a Dying Soul

Several years ago, before my cancer diagnosis, I started playing my violin for people who were sick. This could be in nursing facilities, hospitals, psych units, or even at people's homes. On one such day, I stepped into a bedroom with a four-poster bed and a puffy white comforter. A little head stuck from the top of the blanket.

The woman smoked, completely horizontal, with her face barely visible. A bottle of whiskey sat on her end table, still pretty full. I blinked hard, then stared — so this must be the cantankerous, dying woman who loved the violin.

"You're the fiddle lady?" she said. "You're not what I expected at all. You're much older."

I studied her, then before stopping myself, responded with, "I'm Elisa. And you're not what I expected either. You don't even look like you're dying."

Her daughter, who had led me into the room, turned even paler.

I thought I'd get the smackdown from Old Smoky, who still puffed away at that Camel Gold, but as she studied my apologetic face, she suddenly burst out laughing and coughing and laughing again.

"Awe, kid. You're too honest. But so am I."

I bit my lip and smiled at her. "Mrs. Beck, I like you."

"Yeah, that happens from time to time. I'm usually an acquired taste, but the people who like me right off, I figure those are the good ones." She grinned so wide, showing several missing teeth and a big silver one that modern rappers would go crazy for. "So, what do you got, kid?" she asked.

I lifted my violin from its case. "I'm gonna play some oldies. That's what I heard you like." I snapped my shoulder rest into place and tightened my bow. "Mrs. Beck," I said, because I'm super direct, "you keep calling me *kid*, but you said I'm older than you expected."

"Anyone under fifty is a kid to me. And they keep bringing preteens over to see me—like they're doing a good deed or something. Why are you here anyway, Elisa? Why did you come?"

I thought for a minute. "I guess I just want to make you forget whatever it is you're going through, even if it's just for a minute. Focus on something else and enjoy." I set my violin on my shoulder. "So, I have a favor to ask you. Set down your cigarette and close your eyes."

She kinda snort-laughed, set her ciggy down, then snuggled into that huge white pillow before closing her eyes.

"Now, as I play, I want you to picture a story."

And I started. First, I played the beginning of "Bridge Over Troubled Water" by Simon and Garfunkel. The music started out quiet—a trickle of spring rain. I sang the song's words in my head as I played, causing a whirlwind of emotion to burst from my violin. And Mrs. Beck must've felt it because little tears seeped from the sides of her eyes. She glowed, so utterly beautiful, like an elderly Snow White or something' with her sheared, dyed-black hair and leathery face. But instead of lying there, waiting for the kiss of her prince, she was dying. Waiting for the kiss of God.

Tears heated my eyes too, and I told myself to quit being such a freakin' pansy. I shut my lids. Instead of letting my emotion escape through the weakness in my eyes, I pushed that pain into my arms, my hands, my fingertips. And I played that violin, like a flippin' lover. It cried in my arms, wailing over the melodies and having so much power it reacted to the sheer feeling flooding my body. I knew Mrs. Beck and her daughter could feel the sorrow buried deep in my soul—my sorrow for them. That violin was a magnifying glass, exemplifying exactly why I was there, who I was, and that I wanted to offer at least some semblance of tranquility.

Then my bow grew with deep friction and strength, and I transitioned into notes and melodies that just came to me. My fingers and violin took over. That's the funny thing about me and my fiddle; I *think* I have control, then that thing takes over like an addiction. I have the road map, but my fiddle has the details that always take me there—a good friend, leading me home.

The song swelled, over and over. At one point, a gust of wind rode in through the open window on a high note. Right after that, my fingers and bow slowed to a stop. The notes descended to my D-string, and the weight of the music left my body. The song was over.

I held my violin at my side, that extension of self, then faced the window and closed my eyes. I didn't want Mrs. Beck or her daughter to see me cry. I even prayed the wind would come again, and God would dry my tears. The Becks were sad enough. They didn't need to see some *kid* — over thirty — crying because she "felt bad."

"Elisa," Mrs. Beck rasped. She beckoned me to the side of her bed. I wiped my eyes, then obeyed. She reached out her wrinkled hand, with that soft, paper-thin skin, and grabbed my fingers. "That, Elisa, *that* was beautiful."

"What did you see," I asked, "when you closed your eyes?"

"Something from when I was a kid. Something I thought I forgot. My mom, dad, and I were walking in a field." She took a very deep breath. "I miss them. They were good parents."

I had to twitch my nose just to keep from bawling even more. After all, she'd probably be reuniting with a lot of people soon. I put my violin away, then hugged Mrs. Beck and her daughter.

"It was nice meeting both of you," I said. I left the house and never saw either of them again.

Now that I'm sick, I remember all of these odd moments from my life that have all built into something so much more — proof that I lived.

***

Trey and Indy laughed in the front room, probably getting into some sort of mischief. Instead of going to check on them — and end their fun — I rested on my bed, staring at a massive bruise on my inner arm. "Um, I think it's bubbling," I'd told the nurse as she took labs earlier this week.

"Oh! My hell, Elisa!" she said, seeing my arm swelling up like a cobra waiting to strike. She called out for another nurse, and they pulled the IV as fast as possible. "You'll have some pretty big bruising, and we shouldn't stick you on this side for a while. God, you're so calm—and so nice! I'd be freakin' out. I'm so sorry this happened." She turned to her coworker. "Why does it always happen to the nice ones?"

The whole conversation replayed in my head as I rested in my room. That's when I decided to have a pity party and take a picture. I posed and modeled on SnapChat, trying to get the angle just right so I could send Mike a picture. That's when something huge smashed to the ground in our backyard. Maybe because I tried sending pictures of my bruises to Mike while he was at work.! God apparently doesn't look kindly on people who solicit pity.

The kids and I darted out onto our back deck, so concerned over the noise. A massive part of our tree had blown down in the backyard. It had barely missed our house and our fence.

"Oh, my gosh," I said, then, on instinct, I started laughing. "First water damage," I told Trey and Indy, "then the death of our A/C unit. And now this."

They didn't laugh. Indy looked at me like I'd finally cracked.

I decided to play a game with them from *Pollyanna*. I'd seen that movie with my grandma, and its lesson will never leave me. "Let's play the glad game," I said to my kids, and they both brightened. We've had to play this lots of times. So, here's what we came up with:

No. 1 – At least the tree didn't hit our house.

No. 2 – The repairs to the basement are gonna be awesome!

No. 3 – Mike; Shane, my brother; and Neo, my nephew, already fixed the A/C unit—and I think they had fun doing it. They even went and got death-hot wings after.

So, this afternoon Mike, Trey, and I went outside and took pictures. We figured our family can look at this one of two ways: we lost a great tree or we got some free firewood.

Thank God Mike just built us a firepit.

I might still have cancer, but I'm gonna have s'mores now too.

***

"Elisa?" The woman looked my way, totally dumbfounded. "EC Stilson?" she said louder when I didn't respond.

I didn't recognize this woman at all. But she clearly knew me.

Maybe we'd gone to school together?

She walked over and started telling me all about my life: how my son died and how my dad had colon cancer. She almost went chronologically from the beginning to the end—through my divorce and sickness—saying she couldn't imagine how I've gotten through everything and still "see the bright side." And the whole time I had no idea what to do because I couldn't remember who this woman was!

Finally—getting desperate—I used the oldest trick in the book. "Oh! My gosh!" I squealed. "It's... you!" Then I gave her the biggest hug on earth, hoping that somehow the physical contact would jog my memory.

The woman broke out laughing. "You are just like your books! This is great." Then she laughed so hard I thought she'd bust. "I don't actually know you," she said.

"Wait a minute. Then... how?" It suddenly dawned on me. My life is an open book — well books — plural.

"You did a book signing at my daughter's school, and she won *The Sword of Senack*. We had so much fun reading it that I started reading your memoirs. I just can't believe I would run into you and recognize you from your pictures online and things." She suddenly turned sort of pale. "Oh! Don't think I'm a stalker. I just found a lot of inspiration in what you're going through and how you handle it."

"Don't be embarrassed." I chuckled. "I just hugged you and acted like I knew you!"

"Well, I do feel like I know you. Hey, actually, this is so ironic, but can you do something for me?"

"Um, sure?"

She went to her car and brought back *The Golden Sky* for me to sign. I couldn't believe she had it in her car. This was seriously the oddest — coolest — thing. For once *in my life*, I felt like a successful author.

Life can be so terribly hard. I really don't know if I'm handling it all that well, but moments like this make it pure magic. Even if I can't hold food down and the doctor had to stop cancer treatments for a bit because my liver was dying, even when dinner is burnt, I'm exhausted beyond words, and I make more mistakes than anyone I know, there are Godwinks all around letting me know that God still loves me, and everything will be okay.

I'm still amazed that someone recognized me and actually read my books. But it sure was a neat way to make a new friend. When I started writing, I had no idea how much it would connect me to so many people. If I never would've shared Zeke's story, I don't think I'd have the same amount of support that I have now throughout this cancer diagnosis. There's power in vulnerability—in letting people know what our struggles are. I'm so grateful I've been able to send this message in a bottle out into the world, and that I've made so many new friends—and to still be making memories—along the way.

CHAPTER 34
Wildcards and Breadcrumbs

We often need God's grace the most when we're experiencing the hardest times. As I watched men clearing out our fallen tree today, I felt humbled beyond words.

I was still heartbroken over the tree. We didn't just lose a tree. The hawk that had been watching over me lost its home. Where would he go now? Who would watch over me?

We've struggled through some crazy things lately—and I've wondered how we'd get through all of it. Not only does it feel like everything has broken down in our house, the doctor just told me I can start treatments again in three weeks, but that I might have them for the rest of my life. This feels like a herculean task, but it's the price I must pay to see my children grow up. When I'm not feeling nauseous (or throwing up), I'm taking medications that completely knock me out just so I can keep food down. In short, it's my new normal, and that *needs* to be okay.

I'm not even forty, and I have cancer that isn't going anywhere. End. Of. Story.

We've been dealt some rough hands, but there's another side as well. Just when I think we'll lose the game, we get some crazy wildcard! My brother and nephew helped us fix the A/C in our house. Yesterday, a friend from high school gave us enough money to replace our water-damaged flooring. One of my *amazing* cousins and several friends gave us enough funds so I can continue traveling to Utah for treatments—and everything is currently paid for. And now people showed up to help clear out our tree.

I can hardly believe the miracles I've just seen—it's almost unbelievable.

After the men removed the tree trunk and branches, we ate a dinner they'd brought over. One of the men came to help because his son beat cancer. Another man was a stranger to everyone; he simply showed up because he heard about our situation from a friend.

Everything just came together. It's been really hard needing help, but this generosity made a hard situation surmountable. Today, these people are my miracle.

Today, these people are hawks watching over me.

***

Once I interviewed a Vietnam veteran who told me he'd waded through swamps filled with leeches. He'd smoke cigarettes, and then use them to burn the leeches off so they wouldn't keep sucking his blood.

Melanoma isn't quite *that* bad, but there are days when I do feel like I'm wading through a swamp, just hoping to find solid ground. A friend must have recognized what a rough time I'd been having. She randomly paid for me to get a manicure for Mother's Day, and I've been so excited about it.

But when I got to the salon last week, judgment practically emanated from the woman doing my nails.

She impersonally motioned for me to put my hands on the counter before roughly sanding my nails and yanking on my hands. I tried talking to her, but she acted like she didn't understand English, so we sat in silence for a while.

I'd worn fancy earrings and clothes that day, all from Goodwill, and she hadn't seen that I walk differently. When I'm sitting, no one would know I'm sick. Regardless of the reason why, she didn't act very nice, and I wished I could understand more about her.

It wasn't until she got to my left thumb that she studied my disfiguration and looked at me. "What happened?" she spoke bluntly — in English!

"I cut my thumb in half on a table saw," I said. "It was crazy. The poor kids behind me — blood went everywhere. It was the worst accident that high school wood shop class ever had."

"Humph! And what's this?" She pulled my arm hard and started touching the bruises on my inner elbow.

"I have cancer," I said. "They have to draw my blood a lot and do treatments. I wanted a port, but I guess I can't have one because of other complications."

I swear this woman went from hating me, thinking I was some snotty person, to feeling compassionate.

She showed me all *her* scars then; they ran from her hands to her arms. I couldn't believe I hadn't noticed them before. Just like she'd missed so much about me, I had missed so much about her.

"I'm from Vietnam," she said. "I fished for a living before coming here. These scars are all from fishing." Her eyes twinkled as she let go of my hand and stared at me. "We killed the fish — while they were still alive."

I didn't know how else you'd kill fish, but her words made me smile, as if a real, live pirate sat across from me!

"You have kids?" she asked.

"Yes, I do. Four."

"Ages?"

"Nineteen, sixteen, thirteen, and eleven."

"Nineteen? I have a nineteen-year-old too," she said.

I beamed as she showed me pictures. "She's a real beauty!"

So, we talked about our children, fishing, and even cancer. We agreed how hard life can be and how strange things turn out. And oddly enough, neither one of us could fathom what the other had gone through. I couldn't comprehend Vietnam, and she couldn't imagine having cancer.

And this woman—who'd pretended to not speak English—suddenly became a sort of kindred spirit.

After I tipped her and walked out to my car, she darted from the building and yelled across the parking lot. "Good luck! Hang in there!"

"You too," I said.

It's just nice when we can have these transcendent moments and can find such beauty along the way. I'm so glad I met this amazing woman who felt generous enough to let down her walls to share some of her story with me.

***

While waiting for the nurse to hook me up to an IV, a message came in through Facebook.

An award-winning photographer had seen my "sexy" hospital gown photos I'd posted online—the ones from my mock photo shoot in the hospital bathroom a while ago. She asked to take *professional* pictures of me in a hospital gown for cancer awareness!

"I would love to!" I responded through Facebook I could hardly believe someone wanted to take real pictures of me.

After I'd just gotten set up for my appointment, my sixteen-year-old daughter came to see me.

Things have been hard since she ran away last October, a week before I was officially diagnosed with cancer. I've reached out every single Sunday, just telling her how much I love her, but the responses have been scant until the last couple of months. She randomly started contacting me more and even said she missed me.

I just stared at her during my treatment, thinking how very much I've missed her — and surprised that she'd actually taken the time to come see me. She looked so gorgeous and grown up in a cute, little business dress. I just wanted to reach up to her, hold her hand, and ask her to stay there forever because I need her so much it hurts. She was making a difficult day so much better just by being near me, her mere presence.

Instead, I tried staying strong, and I simply whispered, "You came to see me?"

She nodded, then slowly sat down in the chair next to me.

"This takes a few hours, stay as long as you'd like."

"Sure," she said. And then we'd settled into a sort of silence as we listened to the other patients and family members talking in the partitions beside us.

Sky's absence in our lives has been harder than the cancer. I couldn't understand how we'd gone from extremely close to distant in a matter of moments. It happened right when I got diagnosed, which really made me think. We all knew something was wrong; I'd never been that sick, and I know it shocked my children even before the doctors told us what was wrong.

"Do you still bring a deck of cards with you everywhere?" she asked.

"Yes, I do." I reached into my infusions bag and pulled out a mythological creatures Bicycle deck I'd bought at a gas station. Buying strange decks of cards is my guilty pleasure.

We played games and laughed at a gimpy unicorn on one of the cards. It seemed like old times. At one point, Sky wiped something from the corner of her eyes.

"I forgot how funny I could be," she said, and her words really struck me.

"I didn't forget," I said. "I'll never forget." I patted her hand.

She stayed with me the entire time, and at the end of the visit she asked, "You still want me to come home?"

I nodded. "With everything in me. I just want our family back. I miss you. All of us miss you. Whatever made you leave, we can work through it together."

She actually decided to come home. Now that weeks have passed, I can't tell you how full my heart finally is again. Despite everything we're still struggling through, I am the happiest! Thank God for that visit to the hospital because I think that day is what ultimately encouraged my baby girl to come home.

It's not easy raising teenagers. It's hard being the one to set down rules, make sure they have chores, help with homework and job responsibilities (that five a.m. paper route was the worst!), and work together with your spouse to stay in lockstep. As long as we've shown them how much we love, appreciate, and value them—for who *they* are—it works out in the end. They'll know they can succeed and thrive in this tough world.

This reunion hasn't been completely easy. We've had to talk about my fight against cancer, and she's even spoken with a counselor at the Huntsman.

"I believe she pulled away because she was so scared to lose you," the counselor told me. "She knew you were sick when she ran away—she knew something was wrong. It's pretty common for kids her age to withdraw. It's their way of coping. She said she wasn't close to her father before she ran away. It's probably good she knows what he's like now—she won't have to look back and wonder. But after some of the things she told me about her stay with him, I'm really glad she's back home with you now. You need each other. I'm sorry for everything you've been going through."

"Wow. You'd think cancer would bring families closer together."

"Sometimes it does, and sometimes it doesn't."

I'm still processing all of this, but maybe things are changing in my life. It feels like there's some sort of healing on its way.

***

Dawn, of Fuzzy Love Photography, normally takes pictures of animals, yet she'd sent me an idea of boudoir poses for the hospital gown shoot. I walked into the fancy photography studio, mentally preparing for a unique photo session. Dawn had actually rented the studio for a couple of hours so she could take pictures of me there.

After the insane year I'd had with surgeries, hospital stays, radiation, and infusions—this woman made me feel like a real, live model!

We laughed and had the most wonderful time. I ended up telling Dawn how Sky had run away and come back home.

"I wish I could meet someone who went through this as a teenager—someone who knows what it's like to be so young and have a parent with cancer." I had *just* said the words when the owner of the photography studio peeked her head around the corner.

"I'm so sorry for eavesdropping," she said, "but I heard what you were saying. My mom, well, my mom died of cancer when I was seventeen." Her eyes grew quite large as she waited for my response.

My heart stopped. It became incredibly hard to breathe. There stood this gorgeous business owner who appeared unscathed by hardship, and she was the answer to my prayer.

The studio's owner talked with us about what it was like dealing with this as a teenager and how I should just be as loving and understanding as possible. "I pulled away from my mom too," she said. She hadn't talked much to her mom for the last month before she died.

"I don't blame my daughter for pulling away," I said. "This whole thing is so hard to process. I'm sure your mother felt the same. In the end, we just want our kids to know how much they're loved."

"Your daughter will be okay," the woman said. "She has an amazingly strong mother, and she'll look back and see that—just like I do. Give her the space she needs when she needs it. It'll all work out."

I wiped more tears away.

Dawn and I walked from the building after that. I thanked her for everything. I had a sneaky suspicious she hadn't done this as a cancer awareness shoot at all, but because she wanted to make me feel special.

I gave her a huge hug and asked if she'd like to go to dinner sometime. "You're too much fun," I said before getting into my car.

That's what I did last week after more appointments at the Huntsman in Utah. I had my pictures taken by the best animal photographer in the western states and met a stranger who reminded me that my kids will be okay despite this harrowing situation. They've had a good foundation. God has a plan for my health, and He's also looking out for my family every step of the way.

It's astounding how God can send us breadcrumbs from heaven; after all, when we're open to the unexpected, that's when miracles can happen.

***

I'm a preteen. My sister and her new husband are coming over to visit, and we're all so excited. My mom is singing in the kitchen. My dad is in the backyard, listening to oldies and grilling steaks. He's a construction superintendent who loves being outside in the sun with his shirt off while he's hanging out with our giant Lab.

My brother is on the couch reading a fantasy novel to me. I was listening before getting distracted— thinking about how perfect the moment is. Everyone is so happy. I can feel their joy all around me. I wish I could take a snapshot of the moment, to carry it with me, so it can help me through challenging times in the future.

I close my eyes and think about how perfect life is as my brother reads to me.

"Are you even listening?" he says.

I pretend I'm asleep and start snoring. "Oh. My! Gosh! Are you serious?" My brother walks over to me. He's in his early twenties—and he's my absolute hero. I'm still not sure why, but during those years, he spent so much time with me even though he had all the friends in the world. We played music together, soccer, and he taught me to love writing.

He comes over to see if I'm really sleeping, and I burst out laughing. I can hardly control myself because it's so hilarious that I tricked him.

"Elisa! I knew it!" He lightly smacks me with the book and chuckles.

We help my mom cut veggies in the kitchen. I go say hi to my dad and smile. He's still outside, flipping those steaks, drinking beer, and dancing.

It's such a perfect moment.

Since then, I've had to capture those perfect moments throughout my life. They don't happen very often—and they can be hard to catch—but if you find one, commit it to memory because they're truly precious. I need to make more of these memories with my own kids.

CHAPTER 35
Nature Church and Diner Church

The Edson Fichter Nature Area features a walking path, a watering hole, dog pond, and fishing area. We purchased our house so we could live within a few blocks of the preserve. I used to walk with the kids and bring them fishing quite a bit. I loved carrying our fishing poles and tackle box down the road. People would look at us and smile, and the kids—and our dog, Abby—reveled in every moment of this for the first few months we lived here.

Unfortunately, life got in the way. Indy would ask if we could visit the preserve, back when I was healthy, but I'd always been too tired from working at the newspaper.

"Maybe tomorrow," I'd say, even though I felt fine and probably could've taken on the world.

Now everything seems too late: I exhaust easily, I struggle to walk very far, and I almost always feel flu-like symptoms such as chills and body aches.

This particular day, I wanted to bring the kids to the preserve more than anything, even if the trek to the watering hole killed me. "It'll take a lot out of me, but do you guys want to go to Edson?"

Indy's eyes lit up. "Really? Yes!"

"Ruby? Can you go?"

She shook her head. "Maybe next time." Then she turned to Sky. "We have a lot of clients at the shop today. Call me if you need something?"

"I'll take good care of her," Sky said.

The two of them treated me like I was ninety.

So, after my half-day of work, editing remotely, Trey, Indy, and I donned our swimsuits and grabbed some water.

Sky just smiled. "Are you actually getting in the water?" she asked.

"Maybe."

"You sure you're up for this?"

"Absolutely."

We drove the couple of blocks to the entrance, and then walked into the preserve.

After about two seconds, Trey pointed to some deer on the path. "I swear the deer around here are too comfortable around people."

"I agree," Indy laughed. "But they're so cuddly looking!"

I had to stop often to sit on benches that dot the path. The watering hole is about a quarter mile in— easy for most yet a marathon for me.

Trey and Indy went ahead to scope things out while Sky waited by my side.

"The water is perfect," Trey said when they came back. "And no one is there. This is gonna be the best." He made sure no one could see us, then gave me a huge hug. "Thanks for doing this for us, Mom. We know this is a big deal for you."

I bit my lip and nodded. "Thanks for coming!"

After a few more stops, Sky and I made it to the rope swing where Indy and Trey waited for us.

"Watch this!" Trey said, then ran, grabbed onto the rope, and launched into the water.

"Oh, my gosh!" I squealed as water splashed everywhere. Indy jumped in after him, and the two of them swam around, splashing like puppies.

"Can you help me?" I asked Sky. Then I reached for her hand so I could slowly descend into a flat-rock area where the water pools before falling over itself into a deep canopy of trees.

She held my hand so tenderly but wouldn't step into the water. She worried more about germs than I did.

I felt around with my toes and found solid footing. "Okay! I'm good." I grinned, as the liquid tickled my calves. I couldn't help it anymore, and I sat in the rippling waves that just barely covered my hips, lower back, and legs. "This feels like heaven." I peered around at all the lush plants and the clear, blue water. It seemed truly hard to believe that this Terabithia is right next to our home. "The next day Mike has off, we should make him come here with us."

"Totally," Sky said. "He'd love it here."

She sat down, resting only about a foot away from me on the shore. We stayed like that, lost in time as the waters pooled around me, and Trey and Indy swam in the deeper water just below us.

I could not wipe the smile from my face until Sky turned to me with so much pain glazing her eyes.

"Mom, I don't know if I'll ever forgive myself for what I've done to you," she said, striving to balance her unsteady voice.

"Hey. Hey, what do you mean, kid? It's all good. We're all good."

"It's not, Mom. It's not good. You've been so sick. And I haven't been here for you at all. I didn't respond to your texts. I was just so angry about everything that's been going on. And then so much time passed that I didn't know what to do. And you were still so nice the whole time."

I swallowed hard and decided to ask her something I'd wondered since she's come back. "Sky, do you really think I'm... a bad mom?"

"Wait, what? What do you mean?"

"Some of the texts you sent forever ago," I said. "Especially when I was at the hospital after my back surgery. I remember one night. The nurse had just taken my labs. It was just after midnight, and I was so exhausted. But then you texted me right after that, and I was excited to hear from you. But those messages... they were all about how you thought I was a terrible mother and a terrible person. I didn't even know what to say back. I kept telling you how much I love you. And that I need you. And I'm sorry I've been sick." I started crying so hard, my tears adding to the water around me at the top of the waterfall.

I sighed after a moment. "I'm so sorry to cry. It's not a big deal. It really isn't. I just don't want to be a bad mom, especially when I'm facing all of this. I want to look back and feel like I made a difference, like my life mattered." I tried keeping the sadness out of my voice, but it had become impossible. "It's over now. But some of those messages you sent.... Did you mean all of the things you wrote?" I was babbling now, not even giving her a chance to respond. "I hope you think I've been a good mom. I've honestly tried so hard."

Sky had turned completely pale, the blue waters reflecting off her ashen face. I worried that I shouldn't have brought this up. I'd never want her to look back and feel bad about this time in her life. I live with enough regrets—she didn't need to face a future like that too.

"Mom." She shook her head after a moment, and she seemed genuinely perplexed. "You really got texts like that from my phone, in the middle of the night?"

"Yes. But it's okay, Sky. I just had to ask you about—"

"Dad took my phone around ten every night. He didn't want me staying up on it. And I wasn't responding to you for months. I'm just saying, if you were getting texts from me, especially in the middle of the night, I don't think I was the one sending them."

It felt like a hot knife had gone through my back, right where the bulk of my cancer is. "Wait, what?" I couldn't deal with this stress. The doctor has said I need to avoid thinking about things that upset me because it could make my sickness so much worse. I tried breathing through it, but suddenly the looming court case came to my mind.

Would someone really do that to me? Could these messages be used in court against me, even if Sky were telling the truth and she hadn't sent them? What kind of person would send me those things after I'd just been diagnosed with cancer—after I'd had a surgery so severe it required a blood transfusion?

I shut my eyes, listened to the water, breathed in the air, and just tried not to say anything I might regret about anyone.

"Mom, I've felt bad because I stopped responding to your messages. I just didn't want to face any of this. I'd never say you're a terrible mother, especially while you were at the hospital with cancer. If you really did get texts like that, I am so sorry. That's beyond terrible. Really."

We both remained quiet.

"Mom, I've realized a lot of things about who people really are, and about who really cares about me. It makes this whole thing worse. I'm just so sorry for not coming home sooner. Can you ever forgive me?"

"There is nothing to forgive. We each have to process things in our own way. I ran away when I was seventeen, and you're a lot more like me than you realize. I'm grateful you're here with me now."

I reached up from the water and held her hand again. She cried and cried, letting the moment wash over her. We stayed like that until both of us felt depleted of sadness. And in its place, a newness began.

Trey and Indy eventually came over and sat by me in the waves.

Sky smiled warmly at the kids. "It's so nice being here," she said. "It's so nice being home."

As the cleansing waters washed past my legs, the pain in my back slowly subsided. I closed my eyes and imagined that all the regret, pain, anger, and even cancer would be taken away forever, far past the waterfall and deep into the tumultuous rapids and rocks miles down the Portneuf River.

So much healing needed to take place, but today was truly the beginning. Things just felt different.

"This was the best day ever," Indy said, snuggling her little, wet head into me. "Mom, you make everything so much better."

I hugged her and chuckled. "All of you make life good. I'm so glad we came here today. There really is something special about this place."

We decided to come back to the watering hole at least once a week, so I could build up my stamina, and so Trey can perfect his cannonball.

***

Mike and I went to "diner church" with Trey and Indy. This is basically when we bring the kids to breakfast and talk about a story from the Old Testament.

"I like Noah," Indy said. "Can we talk about the flood?"

But Trey had zoned off, so Mike and I mischievously told a story that directly involved Trey and Indy.

"I want you to imagine that God told Trey to take wood shop class so he could build a huge submarine at the middle school."

"What?" Trey balked. "A submarine?"

"But all of the other kids thought it was crazy! And then two kinds of each animal started coming to the school! And all of the kids were like, what?"

The story continued until Mike made the pipes burst in the school, and it flooded while Trey and Indy stayed safely in the sub with thousands of fluffy animals, which Indy loved.

After Mike read the real story from the Bible, I asked the kids, "What did you learn?"

"That God does stuff to actually help people," Indy said. "He doesn't just watch when we're having a hard time."

"I learned about not giving into peer pressure," Trey said, almost rolling his eyes. "But, I did sorta like the part about the submarine."

"Elisa," Mike said, shutting the Bible, "you've wanted to see the synagogue. Why don't we go?"

It's been a running joke now. Since I announced to friends and family that I don't believe Jesus is the son of God, I've often said, "I believe in the Old Testament. I'd probably make a pretty good Jew." Even if I regret announcing my beliefs to the world, because it made me a sitting target, I guess it helped me sort *some* things out.

"They have services on Fridays," I said. "Today isn't Friday."

We found their schedule online, and it was their annual cleaning day—at that very moment—and the rabbi would be there from out of town!

"You guys want to stop and ask a couple of questions?" I asked.

"I'm staying in the car," Trey said when we got there. He's definitely an independent, strong teenager.

"No, you're coming with us," Mike said.

All four of us nervously edged inside. Only a few people had shown up to help clean and do maintenance on the building.

"God brought you here!" A jolly looking man practically appeared—out of nowhere—then handed us brooms, dustpans, and rags. "Here's the list of what we need cleaned."

Trey looked at me, dumbfounded as two people herded us into a vast meeting area where the massive floor needed to be stripped, swept, and scrubbed.

The first man gave us our marching orders.

"Wait," I said, "we're so happy help, but I have some questions about Judaism and your services."

"The rabbi will come talk to you in a little while."

And he simply left.

So, we did what we'd been told.

Mike scraped plastic from the floor, Trey and I swept, and Indy scrubbed. I can't describe what happened as we quietly worked on that gigantic room, but the kids must've been too stunned to even complain, and after a while, an amazing warmth rolled over me.

It took quite a while, and I'm embarrassed to say I sat down at one point because I felt so weak from the cancer, but just being there seemed so renewing.

The rabbi finally came in. I told him about my cancer. "We love our Baptist church. I'll always bring the kids there on Sundays, but this — coming to find out more about Judaism — is for me."

"The next meeting is Friday. You can come and see what you think."

I told him how it seems like I've been on a beautiful vacation that was supposed to last a month and now it'll be over in a few days. "There's so much left I want to do. But now I have to figure what's most important and what I have time for."

"We're certainly glad you made time to come here today. We really needed the help."

As we drove home, the kids talked about how great it felt cleaning the synagogue. "They even let me paint some of the bathroom!" Indy squealed.

Trey nodded. "Yeah, they actually needed us. I'm glad we went."

I was grateful we showed up when we did. That feeling of renewal, and even healing, as we cleaned, well, sometimes things just work out the way they're supposed to.

CHAPTER 36
Life is an Adventure

Mike and I had looked at shoes and listened to conversations. A skinny girl trudged into the store and didn't have much confidence. She slouched and her eyes darted around the shop.

"Oh, my! Look at you. *You* are beautiful!" Anne, the shop's owner, had said to the girl.

"Me?" She almost stumbled backward.

"Who else? Of course, you! Now get over here. I have a dress for you to try on."

Within minutes, the girl wore a gorgeous flapper-girl dress and hat. The girl glowed as she donned a necklace and appraised herself in the mirror.

"Now, just pull your hair back. That's it! You're gonna model in my fashion show. You know that?"

"Me? But... nobody will want to look at me."

"Oh, yes, they do—and they will!"

The girl had stared at herself and stood even straighter. "Okay," she'd said. "I'll do it."

I'm still not sure if the girl paid a dime, but Anne had made sure she left with one of the most stunning dresses in the shop.

I smiled over the memory. I remembered the black velvet dress Anne had given me for Christmas.

Anne and I had spoken on the phone a few weeks ago, sharing our hopes and fears. Doctors had discovered a tumor in her brain.

"I'm not seeking treatment," she said. "I'm done. I know this is the end."

We cried over the news and then the conversation had changed, and we'd actually laughed about life's ironies. Anne was just like that, always finding the good.

The urge to call her last week became almost overpowering. Of course, life got in the way and I didn't call.

Now I wish I'd taken the time; everything else seems so trivial. Anne is gone.

It's hard to understand why I'm still here and life-changers like Anne had to leave early. I don't know if I'll ever fully comprehend sickness and death.

Anne's memory will live on. I'd never met anyone like her, someone who could drastically change people's lives with a dress and a few simple words.

***

Water doesn't matter if your legs don't work quite right or if your third vertebrae has been removed. You can get in there and feel like a completely normal person.

We've been in Bear Lake for the last few days. My amazing in-laws let us stay at their cabin, so Mike and I could get some time alone for the weekend to relax.

I could hardly wait to visit the beach today—the Caribbean of the Rockies. It took quite a bit of effort to get me into the water, but once there, I practically turned into a mermaid. We swam around, played, and joked.

Some people arrived not long after we did. They grinned at me and Mike as we splashed about. It wasn't until I got out of the water that things changed. An older woman, probably in her eighties, looked at me with such pity as I limped out of the water. My back pulled with intense pain from the cancer, and the sand made my gait appear even worse.

She approached me after Mike left to get my towel.

"Let me help you," she said.

"I'm all right," I said. "I'm really okay."

"But you look like you're in so much pain."

Mike returned at about that time, and I pleaded with my eyes, silently saying, "Get me out of here."

Mike ended up explaining to the woman and her husband, who came up after that, about my cancer and my surgeries.

"I'm so sorry you might be dying soon," the woman said.

I knew she meant well, but seriously? We hadn't said anything about dying, yet this woman seemed willing to dig my grave.

"We better head out," Mike said, seeing my dwindling pride. "Nice to meet both of you."

The woman didn't get a clue and kept talking

Even after I walked away to our beach chairs, I heard her telling Mike, "I can't imagine how hard it must be for her. She's so young. I remember when I had to get my handicapped sticker. That was embarrassing. And to think, I never would've known something was wrong with her until she got out of the water."

I slid my sunglasses on so no one would see my tears.

Mike came over to me. "I'm so sorry, sweetheart. It was hard to get away. She just kept talking."

"I know she meant well," I said after we made it to the car, "but I feel terrible. The pity in her eyes. She didn't even know how to talk to me. And I felt so normal and happy in the water."

Mike and I sat on the cabin's front porch. "I just need to find the good—that always makes things better," I said. "On the bright side, isn't it wonderful how even strangers want to help?"

We stayed quiet for a while, and as we sat there, I remembered a moment from a couple of years ago. I'd gone to the grocery store and scanned items at the self-checkout. A man practically gaped at me. I wondered if something was in my teeth, if my clothes looked wrinkled, if I stood oddly. So many thoughts had raced through my mind as I worried something appeared wrong with me.

Then the man who'd been staring at me came up and asked me out on a date!

"I'm married," I said, "but thank you." And to think, I'd been so self-conscious, paranoid really. Yet now, look at me. Now that something is actually wrong, it's taken some getting used to.

"I need to be grateful things aren't worse," I told Mike. "I just need to embrace this. So what if people pity me. So what if I don't walk the same as I used to. At least I don't need a wheelchair! I don't want some insignificant conversation to ruin my day, especially when that woman meant well. She really tried to be kind, didn't she?"

Mike came over and held my hand. "I'm so proud of you. It must be hard to deal with all of this. And to admit when things are tough."

The two of us eventually decided to get dressed up and go to dinner.

"I love you so much," Mike said after we'd changed our clothes.

"I love you back." I smiled. "Thank you for making today so special. I had fun swimming with you."

Moments later, we walked out the door, so excited for a night out on the town, grateful for each other, thankful for strangers who mean well, and happy to have positive perspectives.

***

Mike and the kids walked around the fun resort town as I waited for our to-go food in the pizzeria.

"This has been a terrible year, and you've been through even more than most," the man said, seeming happy to have made a friend in the waiting area.

"The steroids may give me diabetes. But if I have a shot at life—even with diabetes—it's better than the alternative."

"And you're grateful?" He shook his head. "Let me get this straight. Your liver is failing, you're on the verge of diabetes, and you still have cancer?"

"I'm still alive, aren't I?"

"You really think you can find the good in anything?"

"Or course!" I said without having to think about it.

"Okay. Our food is taking forever. What could possibly be good about that?"

"Well, I got to meet someone new and have a great conversation, didn't I? And I got to sit and rest for a minute."

The man stared at me. "I'm sorry, but I don't even know how to respond to this. It's just that I met the most ungrateful person yesterday, and now I'm meeting the most appreciative woman."

I laughed. "You're just catching me on a good day." I looked at a picture on the wall. "But I do have a lot to be grateful for. If this is my one chance to live, I better make it count."

We stayed quiet, both of us thinking deeply as we waited for our to-go orders at the bustling pizzeria.

"This man I met yesterday," he finally said, "he had it all: a beautiful wife, a fancy car, tons of cash. But when I talked with him, everything was the worst. His wife talks too much. His friend has a more expensive car. He doesn't work because he doesn't need to, and now he's bored out of his mind."

"Seriously? Was this guy for real?"

"Yes! He stayed at a hotel in town, and he couldn't believe the stairs hadn't been vacuumed yet that day."

I tried so hard not to say anything bad because I'd been trying this new thing called keeping my damn mouth shut— *no lashon hara,* as the Jews call it.

"He asked me if I thought he should float the river with his wife. You know what I told him?"

I shook my head. I was beginning to like this stranger. I was trying not to gossip, but nothing ventured, nothing gained!

"I told him he'd hate floating the river."

"But everyone loves the river—once they get out there," I said.

"Are you kidding? Not him. He could find something wrong with Mother Theresa. He'd hate the river."

The lobby door opened, and Mike walked in. "You feeling okay, sweetheart?" He held a little gift bag. Apparently, he and the kids had found something fun at one of the stores.

"Yep. It's been nice resting my legs."

Right after that our order was up, and we paid for our food.

"Your enthusiasm for life is catching," the man said before we could leave. "I'm so glad I got to hear how grateful you are for everything. It makes me feel sort of thankful for all the good things I have too."

"I'm glad." I smiled so big, and Mike and I left.

"Who was that?" Mike asked.

"A stranger," I said. "Isn't it amazing how you can walk into a building not even knowing what exciting thing might happen, then you meet somebody new and have a great conversation?" Mike chuckled as I beamed. "Life is *such* an adventure!"

"Yes, it is," he said.

CHAPTER 37
Hawks and Godwinks

I remembered his words: "You can keep the feather or release into the wind with a prayer. It will find the Grandfathers." Mato-Uste had given me the feather. But every time I released it, the winds brought it back.

"Maybe the Grandfathers are rejecting my prayer. Maybe God is rejecting my prayer." I'd begun wondering if cancer really was a punishment for sins I'd committed in the past. I'd definitely done some bad things, but what made my bad acts worse was that I genuinely knew better.

A bit concerned, I brought the feather home from the cliffs of Arizona and placed it safely on my desk.

Mato-Uste's voice filled with mirth while he talked about the feather. "The Grandfathers are watching out for you, Elisa. That is why the feather stayed."

Although the melanoma in my brain is gone, the cancer grew in my lower back, and the doctors prescribed more radiation. That was around the time a hawk showed up in my backyard. He'd stare at me while I edited on my computer in the kitchen. The two of us would gauge one another. I'd study his beauty, unsure of what he thought of me.

I underwent yet another round of radiation along with grueling sets of immunotherapy that made me lose over fifteen pounds. My liver began failing after that.

"The treatments are trying to kill the cancer and your liver," the doctor said as I sat in the hospital, enduring steroids and more testing. The whole time, I wondered how my family had handled the news. Maybe the hawk looked after them while I could not.

After they released me from the hospital, the doctors halted all treatments. "You need your liver," one specialist said. "We can't continue treatments unless your liver heals. Even then, it will be a balancing act. Unfortunately, you're living through a very uncertain time right now."

When I got home, I didn't see my hawk. Instead, the summer heat became almost unbearable with deadly dry winds. That's when the hawk's tree fell over. This made me feel like all hope was lost. The hawk had been a sign that someone looked out for me. But where would he perch now with his favorite branch gone?

I worked facing the deck last week, wondering if I'd ever see my hawk again, when one, then two hawks landed on another branch in my backyard. Then three and four hawks!

I went outside. Instead of flying away, each of them turned to meet my gaze. That night, they began building a huge nest. Once again, they landed on separate branches so they could turn and look at me. We cocked our heads and studied one another. After a while, they went back to building.

Those birds gave me so much peace. Whether it was just because they like our yard or because they were actually looking out for me, I was grateful they were here. Strange that they came back shortly after I started treatments again, and the doctors said they're hopeful we're on the right path for fighting this cancer.

Sometimes it seems all hope is lost. Your hawk might not stick around when you expected. Something as stable as a tree might crash down in your life, but that leaves room for greater miracles. The best things can happen when we rise from the ashes instead of staying stuck in the mire.

***

Another friend died totally unexpectedly. This is yet another death since doctors told me last year that *I* would be the one to die soon. It was devastating — and shocking. This person had been supportive and concerned about my death. Now, he's gone and ironically, I was still here, staring at the hawks in my tree.

I thought the hawks building a nest might forecast hope.

"Maybe it's a sign," I said to my husband. "Or maybe it isn't. What do you think?""

Mike looked at me seriously. "I'm the wrong person to ask, Elisa. You know what I believe."

He's a hilarious, life-of-the-party guy who doesn't like labels — especially the word atheist. People hear it and don't quite grasp what it encompasses — or they hear it and judge negatively. He prefers nonbeliever.

I pried further despite knowing the answer.

"No, sweetheart. I'm so sorry, but I don't think it's a sign," he said.

A strange fear overtook me while a new pain ran the length of my body. The pains have been getting worse again lately, a sobering fact. In that moment, feeling those pains again, my legs weakened.

I sat to look at the hawks once more and whispered, "Maybe Mike is right. Maybe this isn't a sign. I just want some confirmation that I'll get better."

I sighed. These signs— Godwinks—are what I hold on to. Mike is so strong he doesn't look for confirmation, but I need some type of reminder that despite the suffering and pain of life, God is looking out for all of us. Signs that everything will be okay, and God will protect me even in life. Even in death.

As I gazed out the back window, rain splattered the glass, a final collision after its long descent through the sky. The water scattered, tendrils fighting to reach the dignity of the ground. My thoughts turned to the hawks. How would they fare in the rain?

Four hawks had quickly flown right next to the nest. They made a circle, held their wings out, and bent over the formation of twigs and sticks. The winds rocked the birds. The rains beat against them. And instead of leaving, the majestic creatures practically weaved themselves together and leaned farther over the nest. They would do anything to provide protection.

I anxiously grabbed a cup of coffee and continued watching this show—far better than anything on Netflix. The storm ended shortly after it started. The hawks didn't leave until the rains and wind stopped. I exhaled.

Seeing that they'd saved the nest brought me a renewed sense of peace. I'd never seen something like it. Ever.

"You okay, sweetheart? You want more coffee?" Mike asked after walking in and seeing my empty mug.

"I'm good. I'm just thinking about signs and how I think those hawks do symbolize protection."

"They very possibly could," he said, conceding to what I needed to hear. Then he smiled down at me kindly. He's the most wonderful man, really.

CHAPTER 38
The Forgiveness Card

"Today just isn't working for me," I told Mike.

He looked a bit worried because normally every day works for me—every day is "the best day ever."

"I'm worn down," I said. "It's just hard not seeing an end to being sick, ya know? It's so daunting. I just don't know when the pain will stop."

"That's it. We're doing something fun."

"Like what?"

"I'm bringing you to Goodwill." He waited for me to smile—because I love a bargain—then he went on. "I'll pick out an outfit for you and you'll pick one for me. But it has to be some sort of theme. Like a profession. A doctor or a teacher or... something. And then we'll go out like that."

Even though it was a rough day, I laughed. "I'm exhausted, but who could pass up a date like that? It's a deal!"

At Goodwill, I had no idea what to get for Mike until I passed by some suspenders. "Yes!" I whispered under my breath. I could dress Mike like an old man. I grabbed the suspenders, a plaid shirt, some faded jeans that came in tight at the ankles, a pair of glasses, and a hat.

When we got back to the house, so we could change before going out, I could hardly wait for our outfit exchange.

"Oh, my gosh!" he said. "You're dressing me like... an old man! I should've known."

"And what am I supposed to be?" I asked holding up a studious jean dress.

"A teacher's assistant."

After we donned the clothes, we immediately got into character. Mike talked like an old man—a bit exaggerated if you ask me. He even called me "Sonny." And I seriously had the best time.

At the end of the night, I realized I hadn't felt self-conscious as I walked or inadequate. Instead, I'd been so happy to simply be with the man I love.

"Mike," I turned to him, "I just want you to know how thankful I am for you and everything you've done for me and the kids this last year. I don't know anyone who would handle this as well as you have." After all, he's cooked, taken care of our family, helped me, and made sure all of us were happy. "I'm just so lucky. It's hard being sick, but you make it all better somehow. I can't imagine if our roles were reversed. I don't think I would've handled it half as well." Then the thought was too much. "I can't stand the thought of you suffering. I hope you'll always stay healthy, and carefree, and young."

He peered over at me, his eyes squinting. "What are ya talkin' 'bout, darlin'. I'm a hun-dred yeeears old."

I giggled through my tears and hugged him. "Whatever you are, you sure are the best at it."

***

I sat, completely stunned. The Hebrew words wrapped around me like a balm, and I faintly heard the haunting harmonies my violin could play on top of the alluring melody. Like a child running to the Pied Piper, I closed my eyes, yearning for the glory of God.

The music ended, and the rabbi gave a few people cards. Of course, I'd somehow been one of the chosen volunteers. I turned the paper over curiously to read a single word.

FORGIVENESS

Why had I been given *that* card? I wanted a redo. I strained to look at a card someone got in front of me. Patience? Forgiveness and patience aren't things I excel at. Well, theirs wasn't much better. Good luck, buddy!

"I've given a few of you cards," the rabbi said. "Please, one at a time, tell us about an experience when you've embodied the word on the card."

I quickly handed the forgiveness card to Mike. "Looks like you're up," I whispered.

"Um...." Mike's eyes bulged.

"Mike, I have cancer. Please."

"Oh, my gosh. Don't use that again. That's not even fair!"

As he studied me, I suppressed my laughter. "Fine!" I whispered.

At that point, a man who looked like Jesus walked into the synagogue and sat by me. We looked at each other awkwardly. He knew this was a synagogue, right? Then, I broke eye contact and stood.

"Oh, yes! Thank you!" the rabbi said, clearly relieved that someone had decided to talk about their card.

"My card is forgiveness."

"Is there a time when you've shown forgiveness?" he asked.

"Well, I hope it's not too much to share, but I have cancer. Stage four melanoma. The doctors initially gave me two years to live, and now I might have more. But death, well, even though we all face it, when you've been told you'll die soon, you have to make peace with a lot of things. There are people I've wronged and people who have wronged me. I've been forgiven and offered forgiveness, but it's not always in the ways I've expected. Sometimes it's through giving time and rebuilding relationships to what they should've always been. In that way, cancer has been a gift. I have the chance to make peace—which comes from forgiveness—before I die." Then I sat down. Someone else talked about their card: positivity. Another person stood and shared a story about love.

The modern-day Jesus kept staring at me. I felt uncomfortable until the service ended, and it was time to mingle. Still, the guy followed me after a moment, even as another congregant showed me the Torah scroll at the front of the church and made Mike hold the heavy thing over his head just so he could "get a feel for it."

"Some people hold this over their heads while other people pray. It's heavy enough that you hope it'll be a quick prayer," the congregant said.

"Wow! That *is* pretty heavy." Mike laughed.

Someone tapped my shoulder. The modern-day Jesus stood there. Then he asked to talk with both me and Mike, but his voice strained as if he'd lost part of his tongue or been born with a severe oral defect.

"Hello." I forced aside my concerns. "My name is Elisa. It was a lovely service, wasn't it?" I smiled brightly as I shook his hand. "It's my first time being in a physical service like this, not just on Zoom."

"Y...y...yes, it was ni...ce," he stammered, slowly explaining how he wanted to speak with me after he heard what I said about cancer and forgiveness.

"Do you mind if I sit down?" Mike and Jesus made a space so I could sit next to them. "My back and leg always give me trouble if I stand too long. Sorry about that. What would you like to talk about?"

He explained that he'd been such a dynamic speaker, he'd decided to become a Christian pastor. "I w...www...went to Texas." He'd gone to school and almost gotten his PhD in Texas when he was diagnosed with cancer. It first appeared as a tumor in the roof of his mouth. A surgeon removed it, but this man would never talk the same again. Tears filled his eyes. "I didn't ev...ev...even finish getting my PhD. What was the point?"

"But why?" I asked. "You have such a story to share. You have so much to say."

"I ju...st don't kn...know. Who w...wants to listen to someone like this?" He held the back of a pew so tightly his knuckles whitened. "Anyway, I don't know exactly what you... what you are go...going through, but I do know it's hard." He said they got all the cancer and he's in remission now. "But this is how I'll... I'll live now."

He'd come to a Jewish synagogue in Idaho while visiting family. Something inspired him to attend the service that night. He'd felt like he needed to hear my story about forgiveness and perseverance as much as I'd needed to hear his story about remission. "Don't... don't lose hope," he said.

I bit my quivering lip, and Mike held my hand as the man looked at us.

"I'm glad you're in remission," Mike said.

After a moment, silence rested among us like an old friend, and oddly enough, a type of understanding descended as well.

"Th...thank you for let...letting me talk with you."

"I hope you'll finish getting your PhD," I said. "You'd make an amazing pastor. Who knows the lives you might change? I know we'll never forget you."

Mike nodded in agreement.

Before he left, a huge smile lit his face. "Thank you," he said.

"No, thank *you*," I said. I thought about his words, as he left, and I knew we were meant to hear each other's stories.

***

We'd planned a fancy girls' trip to a resort town, so when Dee called the night before and canceled her trip from Missouri for health reasons, although I understood, I felt pretty devastated.

"It's nonrefundable, Dee. I don't know what to do." I delivered the bad news. "But Mike and I can pay you for the hotel. That way you're not out the money." We're strapped for cash because of cancer treatments, but she didn't need to house the cost, especially after dealing with her own health issues.

"Elisa, why don't you and Mike just go and enjoy it. You've both been under so much stress, and I know you don't get much time alone. This is on me."

"But—"

"Elisa, this is what I want."

"I still wish you could be here," I said.

We'd planned so many fun things. Eating cheese pizza and talking about philosophy and religion. We'd watch movies and play old games together. I'd even planned to let her win a few times! (Insert sarcasm — that woman wins at everything.)

"You'll have fun. And you'll also get that fancy dinner I paid for. One of you will have to eat the vegetarian meal, but what the heck." A bit of excitement laced her voice, and I wondered if she'd actually planned this whole thing.

Mike and I entered the rustic hotel and prepared for dinner. I blended my smoky eyeshadow and glued on false eyelashes, then slipped into the tub to shave my legs — a battle since both cancer and surgeries left part of my right leg numb.

I finished up, then donned a dress I'd found at Goodwill and some pearls from Walmart.

Mike — that giver — had me model in front of the restaurant, and I smiled because despite everything, he makes me feel like I'm worth something. "Tilt this way. That's it. Look down." It wasn't until we entered the restaurant that things flew south for the winter.

Mike peered around, appreciating the antique decor and delicious food in front of us.

The ladies at the table to our left began gossiping. Of all the things God's gifted me with, my kids hate my super-hearing.

"Look at that dress. It must have cost a fortune. And that hair — the latest fad."

"And those pearls!"

"Some of the people who come here," another woman said. "They know how to make money and how to spend it. But few of them appreciate what really matters in life."

"Cheers to that."

My hand nonchalantly went to the three-dollar imitation pearls around my neck. My dress had cost five dollars. My hair is only a couple of inches long after finally starting to grow out after radiation. (Thank God the bald spots are gone!) But were those ladies seriously talking about me?

"What do you think he does for a living?" a woman in a blue dress asked.

"Who knows. He was probably born with a silver spoon in his mouth. I bet they're from California."

"Hey, I'm from California," another woman said, and they broke out laughing.

I turned to Mike, wondering if he'd heard any of it. But he has a skill I need to harness: blocking out the bad, a.k.a. gossipy people, and only taking in the good, antique decor.

I felt small and dirty as I looked down at my shoes, hair gleamed in the candlelight. I'd missed a large section of hair *by my right ankle*! Feeling like a hairy Esau, I sighed in disgust. I couldn't even shave my legs right—or go into a restaurant without people gossiping about me.

"Oh, my God," Mike said. "You look pale, Elisa. How are you feeling?"

Like Esau! "Honestly, I'm struggling," I whispered, hoping he wouldn't see the forest on my right leg.

He gave me some medicine, which I swallowed with a drink of water from a wine glass—classy.

"What happened?"

"Nothing," I lied. But stress exacerbates everything. And while listening to those loose-lipped women, my spine tensed until the pain became almost unbearable. "I'll be fine."

Mike pulled out a deck of cards and we played a few games. I won, so I forgot about judgment and cruel words.

Our waitress came out and she scanned the cards that *did not* belong in a place like that. She grinned.

I don't know how, but we ended up telling her the story about Dee paying for our hotel and dinner. "I have cancer," I finally said so loudly the women next to us stopped talking and one of them dropped a fork. "We're here—at this fancy place—because she did something so nice for us."

"We've been through some hard times," Mike said, "and I didn't even realize how much we needed a break."

When the meal ended, Mike helped me from my seat. I hunched more than normal from the pain and the hard, antique chair.

"I would've never known," a woman said as I limped forward.

"Poor, poor, beautiful soul. She's so young."

I looked at them sadly. "Knowledge changes perspectives, doesn't it?" I said to Mike, but the women must've known I'd said it for their benefit, and each of them turned blood red.

"Thank you, Mike," I said as he helped me walk toward the door.

"Did you have a good time?" he asked.

"The best! The food was amazing! And the dinner itself was unforgettable. How did you know to pull out those cards when you did?"

"You just looked like you needed to lose at something."

Maybe he had heard the women.

***

"She never went to Europe."

"She didn't take a long trip on a train or go canyoneering."

"She never finished learning Italian."

Then these people—the critics of my life—turn brutal.

"She never saw her kids grow up."

"Or got to watch them graduate from college."

"She didn't see them get married."

"And she never grew old with Mike."

I want to tell these people to shut up. Be quiet! But I'm stuck. I'm in an open casket, with satin and flowers all around. They've tried to make death beautiful so it's less scary. But that death box isn't what's holding me back from telling them off. I'm dead, still trapped inside my decaying, inadequate body. *That* holds me back.

"Sweetheart? Sweetheart!" My husband shook me, and I threw my arms around him.

"I'm having that dream again—where I'm stuck in my body. And everyone is making me remember the things I never did. I didn't see the kids grow up, Mike." I sobbed so hard. "I didn't get to see it!"

He held me for the longest time, then whispered, "I found something awesome in the hotel room, and I want to show it to you."

I opened my eyes, wiped away my tears, and looked around at the fancy bed and breakfast Dee had paid for. Mike and I should be enjoying how beautiful it is. I didn't have time for nightmares and dumb reminders that I have cancer. This was supposed to be fun.

Mike pointed to a vase. "Look inside."

"I can't. Don't you remember? I said it looks like an urn. No more reminders of death."

He shook his head. "Come on, Elisa."

I opened the lid and found a note inside. "What kind of person would leave a note like this in a hotel vase? Do you think there are more?"

Mike excitedly rifled through various items in the room.

"I don't think you should be—" I began, but he found more notes and piled them on the floor.

I gingerly lowered my body to the ground, and Mike pulled a pillow from the bed. He cradled me right there on the floor, and we read note after note, discovering stories from people who had been married for decades and couples who'd spent their wedding night in that very room. We read three letters written to a man named Scott from three different women.

"Do you think Scott is bringing different women here?" Mike asked. "Are they all talking about the same guy?"

"Maybe so." I forgot about my dream and smiled as we read the letters addressed to Scott again. "We have to write a letter and leave it in the room."

"I'll leave that up to you," Mike said.

"I can't wait to start it with 'Dear Scott.'"

Mike laughed.

Afterward, we put all the notes back where he'd found them.

It wasn't until the afternoon, while Mike busily packed, that I wrote a note. But it wasn't about what I hadn't accomplished in life. Instead, I wrote about my amazing children and family, who have filled my life with such joy. I wrote about being an author and playing the violin. I described what it was like finally knowing what made me tick.

And then, I wrote about Mike. "As a single mom of four kids, I prayed God would send me a miracle.

He sent Mike, the kindest person I've ever met. We spent the night in this hotel because I needed a momentary escape from cancer. Some days are good, and some days are terribly bad. The point is that if you're reading this, I hope you'll appreciate every moment. At the end of your life, don't regret what you didn't do. Instead appreciate the memories you've made and the people you're lucky enough to have known. That's it, really. It's all about doing the best you can and being grateful."

After signing my first name, I went to hide the note in a large box on the mantel, and I noticed Mike has left one there too.

I opened it, read the words, and smiled. He'd written a note that closely mirrored my own.

Someday, someone else will read our words of love—surprised to find notes at a special bed and breakfast in Idaho.

***

It feels selfish to keep his broken body alive. But still, as the nurse wheels my son into the room, I ask, "What if I changed my mind? What if I can no longer take him off life support?"

She shakes her head sadly and explains it was too late. No matter how much I want my baby to live, the process for him to die has begun.

I hold him. He has the strongest little hands and such soft brown hair. My poor, sick baby—he is so perfect to me.

I don't want to watch, but my eyes stay glued to his every detail as he suffocates in my arms, breathing oddly, gasping for air—like a goddamn fish. He snuggles into me, asking for help, but I can't do anything to save him. In fact, his death is my decision. My fault. Now I have to watch him die.

I naively think a miracle will happen *then*. God knows I have enough faith. This could be like John 4 when Jesus heals someone's son from afar. But this isn't some story in the New Testament. This is life. If it's time for someone to die, no one can tempt fate's hand.

After an eternity of labored, sporadic breathing, my son turns blue despite all my hopes. And my baby boy dies.

I shook myself from the memory and turned to the nurse. "I feel like I always have the flu."

"You might feel like that for a long time," the nurse said. "It's just part of this journey with cancer. At least we have pain medicine."

"I really don't like medicine," I countered, but this is the new normal they keep talking about. I sighed. "And now I might need radiation on my neck and throat?"

"Right. We'll do scans to confirm though. We need to see if there's any growth."

"And there's a chance it could affect my ability to talk normally and to sing?"

"Yes, but like the doctor said, if you do need radiation again, it will most likely shrink that tumor. That's the good news."

I didn't mean to, but I let out a little laugh. I've been working so hard to speak no evil—*lashon hara*. Apparently, more radiation could make that easier.

"But I love to sing," I said, trying to keep from crying in front of a stranger. I couldn't imagine not being able to sing in concerts like I used to or staying silent during worship at church. Sometimes all of this was just too much to carry.

Then I return to that memory with my son.

I want to change everything and keep him on life support. I *want* to be selfish and keep him alive not because he should live in pain. Because I *need* him.

"Elisa. Elisa?" the nurse stepped closer. "Are you okay? I know this news about the radiation must be hard."

"You know, if I didn't have a young family, I don't think I'd continue with treatments. There are just so many things I'm losing to stay alive. I don't mean to sound ungrateful. I know other people have it so much worse, but right now — for me — this is hard."

She left the room after a moment and the door shut. I stayed even though I should have packed up. And despite everything, I suddenly understood the situation with my son. I knew — beyond doubt — that I did the right thing by letting him go. This pain I've been suffering through is only a taste of what he endured.

I thought then about how continuing treatments is the hardest thing I've ever physically done.

No matter the outcome of this situation, everything would be okay. There must be true beauty in the good and the bad.

***

Even when my son died, he could feel my love wrapped around him as his soul prepared to enter heaven. I'm just so grateful I got to be with him before he embarked on a new journey without me.

Now I must find a strength in myself I never knew I had. Plus, I really think my son is rooting for me—all the way from heaven.

Even if cancer robs me of everything else, I hope it will never take my ability to find the good. Right now, that's the best I can hope for.

CHAPTER 39
What are You Fighting for?

"My name is Jay." The tan man smiled. I could picture what he probably looked like years ago as a surfer, before cancer got to him. "I have stage four bladder cancer. You?"

"Stage four melanoma," I responded.

"You look pretty good for having cancer," he said.

"So do you." I grinned. "What can we say? We're awesome!"

He chuckled then started talking about his tumors, referring to them as "these guys."

"Look at this rash," he said, "and all these scabs I keep getting. It's crazy what we go through to keep on livin'. And the whole time, these guys just keep eating away at my body. I've been fighting this dang thing for eight years—"

"Seriously? I can't imagine eight years. I've been dealing with mine since last year, and I'm already tired."

"You're so strong though," he said. "I can see it! And you're positive. You have exactly what you need to get through this." He told me about all the drugs and trials he's been on. "It's amazing I'm still here. They told me I was gonna die when they first diagnosed me. So, don't lose hope, kid."

"What are you fighting so hard for?" I asked. "What's your reason?"

"I want to see my granddaughter grow up."

I nodded. "I want to see my kids grow up too." We stayed quiet for a moment. "You know," I sighed, "I had the strangest dream that I bargained with death. I always wanted more years, and then just a few more years. Until it had been decades and my body was sick beyond repair."

"Ain't that the truth. Your dream was right. We always want more."

A nurse came around the corner and said it was time to go back.

"Wait," Jay said, "I need to tell you something important."

"Okay?"

"I thought I beat this thing." His eyes pleaded with me as the words left his mouth. "I had three good years when I knew I should travel and do all the things I'd always wanted. But I put it off, and now the cancer is back. I worry I'm getting really close to the end."

I wanted to hug him, tell him he could still take those trips. But his elbows were far too bony, and his legs looked frail beyond comprehension. After eight years, his fight was almost over.

"I'm just saying if you ever feel up to it, do those things. Take those trips. Don't let anyone hold you back. Don't have those regrets, like I do. When you feel good, just live."

I went back to an hour-long MRI, and the whole time I thought about the spunky man I'd met in the waiting room. I sure hope I'll see him again.

CHAPTER 40
Fiddler on the Lot

A guy is playing violin in the Fred Meyer parking lot. You should come join him.

My friend's text made me smile because she knows me well.

"Hey," I yelled to my kids in the other room, "wanna go on an adventure?"

Only Sky sounded remotely interested, so we grabbed my fiddle, hopped into Sky's car, and eventually found a woman by a violin case in the Fred Meyer parking lot.

"You want to jam?" I asked with so much excitement.

"No English," she said. "Italian."

Sky and I were *made* for moments like this! We've both been taking Italian lessons, so we told her we speak a little Italian.

Unfortunately, we couldn't understand much of what she said. I pulled out my phone and used Google Translate.

We all conversed that way, typing questions and answers into the translator on our phones — and it was kind of fun! Then, things got serious.

They'd fallen on challenging times, so now, they were standing in this parking lot, asking for help as her husband fiddled for tips. And to think, this brave woman couldn't even speak English.

Right before we got there, her husband had left to see a mechanic because their car had broken down. She had health problems on top of everything. And, they didn't have enough money for rent.

I typed back, "I'm so sorry. I don't know exactly what you're going through, but I understand that life is hard. I have cancer, and I came to see you to get my mind off things by helping someone else."

As she read the Italian translation, she started crying and asked if she could hug me. So, we stood there, hugging and crying in the parking lot. Sky just looked at us and smiled.

I asked if I could play a song for her.

As the notes crescendoed, the winds seemed to shift, and the weather didn't have the same bite to it.

I hoped — with everything in me — that this change symbolized a better future for this sweet woman and her family.

I packed up my violin, and although Sky and I didn't have much to give, we left the woman with what we had.

"*Buona fortuna,*" I said.

"*Grazie.*" She beamed, and we left her there, standing with her sign, still asking for help.

I hope the winds of change will find her. Maybe they'll find both of us.

***

Our twenty-year high school reunion was in a few weeks, but my friend couldn't make it, so they came all the way from Washington, DC, to see me anyway. I could hardly believe how great it was to hang out, but I wanted to make a memory neither of us would ever forget.

"Will you walk up Main with me?"

"Sure!" my friend said, grinning.

I planned to jump in with every band we passed. What was the worst that could happen?

Cancer has robbed me of a lot of dreams. Last year, I had to stop fiddling at gigs because I couldn't stand for long anymore. I didn't even have the stamina to sit for more than a few hours. I couldn't drive far to reach an audience. And lately, even some old songs on the radio would cause a sadness in my heart that I couldn't quite explain.

We traversed Main. The first band didn't seem enthused to see me, so I played quietly as we skirted by.

I tried fighting a sadness that threatened to overwhelm me. Maybe my time with music had passed, just like my life was passing. Those glorious musical moments were gone.

As we stood in an audience surrounding another band, the bassist looked out and smiled. "Hey, fiddler!" he said, pointing to me.

Was the bassist of Rail City Jazz seriously pointing to me?

"Get up here!"

I excitedly went on stage, and those Samaritans gave me a solo. I could've cried as we played. They had no idea what a kind thing they'd just done for someone who'd been losing hope.

A couple of weeks later, I checked their Facebook page.

"Friends," their latest post read, "it saddens us to announce that Brady Meline, Phillip's wife, died on Sunday after many years of suffering."

I nearly dropped my coffee. I frantically found her obituary and discovered she too had battled cancer.

I shut down my computer and stared out the window, stunned that they'd just helped a stranger with cancer, right before losing someone to the same dreadful disease.

***

Will my life end like an unplugged clock or the slow decline of a poorly wound watch? I wondered this as we drove up the canyon to my high school reunion.

A table rested there, clad with photos and memories from the fourteen class members who have already died (two from cancer and twelve from drugs or suicide). According to some doctors last year, my picture would be on that table for the next reunion. There's something about a predicted death: It's haunting.

I worried these thoughts might overshadow the night, but after Mike and I arrived at the reunion, so many wonderful surprises waited for us. Mike taught some friends of mine how to do the lawnmower dance, the sprinkler, the shopping cart, and the sea walk. He drank smuggled booze from a backpack concealed under the table, bonded with one of my favorite friends from back in the day, and got hit on by someone who came across the room just to meet him.

And as people hugged me and said hello, a jolt of love catapulted me back into the moment. I felt real pride for a friend who followed his dreams and became a well-known chef in Park City. I beamed as a woman talked about her children. And I felt true excitement while making a new friend who recently moved home to be closer to their kids.

That one girl was there, you know, the one who gets even prettier with time. The smartest kid in school talked about his epic software job. The school nerd seemed to be the only one filling out high school bingo, and of course, there was the one guy who still doesn't know my name.

But I was happy to show Mike off and remember again how important it is to live in the moment. I reconnected with some legends and made plans to see them again soon. I could hardly wait to hear more of their stories, taste some gourmet food, and go to coffee with people who only got better with time.

It was an unforgettable night—especially when Mike told someone he'd taken chemistry with them. Nothing like having an impostor at my own reunion.

CHAPTER 41
Tie Up a Life

"Hello?" my lawyer's voice boomed on the other end of the line. "Elisa, something big has happened. I need you to check your email." His voice crackled. "El— Can you hear—" Then my phone dropped the call.

"Who was that?" Mike asked.

"The lawyer," I mouthed in the front seat.

"We don't have great service up here. Maybe you can call him when we reach Butte?" Mike asked.

We'd taken the kids on a spur-of-the-moment road trip and even flipped a coin to see which direction to go. We'd all been pleasantly surprised to find ourselves in Bannack, Montana, an infamous ghost town.

"This is awesome!" Indy almost howled from the back seat.

We paid the visitor fee, then immediately began walking through an area that was first part of the Lewis and Clark Trail in 1806 before being declared the First Capital Territory of Montana in 1864.

I kept thinking about the call from the lawyer. What had he wanted? It must've been big news about the case. But it wouldn't do me any good to stew about it now. I shook off any thoughts and worries about court and custody of the kids and brought myself to the current moment. This is a skill I've had to master.

"Mom, this is seriously so cool," Trey said next to me as we both walked into a decrepit hotel.

"Let's go there." I motioned, and he followed me up a spiral staircase. "Trey," I faced my handsome boy who's turned into a young man overnight, "I hope you and the girls will always know how amazing you are. You make life shine so bright for both me and Mike. I am so lucky that I get to be your mom."

He grinned. "I know how much you guys love us. We *all* know."

I glowed with so much happiness. After going through everything that I have, that acknowledgment is the very best I could hope for; the culmination of everything that's been important in my life is knowing that my loved ones understand how much I care about them.

Trey turned and stared out the window then. I followed his gaze, wondering who had been there before us, and I felt proud to be introducing my thirteen-year-old son to a real part of history.

But as I looked out the window, a strange memory hit me from ten years before. A proprietor purchased an old building in Deadwood, South Dakota, where Butch Cassidy himself allegedly visited. The owner asked me to play my violin in the upper level, and a strange song had come to me. With every note I could almost see the old drapes materializing and a newly shined floor suddenly gleaming. People played cards, laughed, and fought rising tempers.

I remembered and reminisced. But what's odd is that as I stood with Trey in Bannack, Montana, another song came to me, a sweeping melody.

I'm still not sure why, but I started singing it, slowly, surely, and I could almost imagine the town, rife with excitement. The street filled with colorful characters; horses corralled down the road. I could envision it more vividly with each note. I was there — in my imagination — and it *was* beautiful.

Then Trey clutched my hand. "Mom! Stop. Stop singing." He said shadows shifted and light had moved down the hotel's hallway.

So, Trey and I left the nearly two-hundred-year-old hotel and joined our family who stood outside of the building. We visited a cemetery after that, where the oldest person buried there was born in 1809.

"It's strange what they put on the headstones," Trey said. "Doctor. Preacher. Daughter of Mr. Matthew Peat...."

"It is strange! How people choose to identify themselves, especially at the end. It makes you wonder, what gives your own life meaning. It's clear what gave them meaning."

I looked at him so proudly. He's such a deep-thinking young man. I know something truly "good" and "kind" will define him.

Then we left. And it wasn't until the next day that I became hospitalized in Bozeman — the closest town with a medical facility. "You're lucky you came in when you did," the doctor said. "You have sepsis — an infection in your blood. You'll be just fine now. But you shouldn't be sitting in a car, driving all over the place taking road trips — you need to be resting in bed and trying to get better."

I heard his words and they stung. To not be able to take road trips and do something that simple to have fun with my family seemed miserable. So, after visiting hours ended, and I sat alone in the hospital room, I instantly thought about the ghost town and all those old graves. Is this a sign that my life is winding down to a close? I know it's not my time yet—and hopefully won't be for a long time—but when it is, what will define me? What set of words will tie up my simple life?

And something else bothered me too. I hadn't had a chance to call my attorney. What in the world had he needed to tell me?

CHAPTER 42
Progress is Progress

Tuesday night, after a horrendous bout with sepsis, I felt like I was in a whirlpool, getting sucked into some inescapable vortex where I could never get out again. I'd had more pains recently. They think it might not be from cancer this time. It might be this infection my body has been battling!

This is such a strange journey dealing with cancer and all the effects of treatment too. It's not these blips that are so terrifying, it's the recovery after. Like a pair of thawing feet, beating and throbbing back to life, each deadly moment only seems especially horrendous as I'm recovering.

I think I've handled all of this quite well, but on this day, I did not.

Visitors were restricted due to COVID-19 concerns. A CNA mistook me for a surgical patient (probably because of how I walk) and put an alarm on my bed so that if the weight changed, she could put me back in bed. As the room darkened around me, the walls surged closer, and everything collapsed in on me. I thought about the removal of my L3 vertebrae (and how torturous that had been), the liver failure (and constant vomiting and severe weight loss), the court case over custody of my kids, and now the sepsis (more painful than anything before). Stuck in debilitating fear, I had a panic attack.

My hand shook as I hit the call button, and luckily my nurse, not the CNA, came in. She turned the weighted alarm off on my bed (since I was actually an ambulatory patient), walked me down the hall to a nice chair, and even gave me black tea in a little Styrofoam cup. "I'm so sorry you're going through all of this. I can't even imagine."

She left me there for as long as I wanted. I pulled out my phone and put on whatever breathing exercise I could find on YouTube, closed my eyes, and listened.

The next day, Mike came to see me first thing, and I threw my arms around him and never wanted to let go. He brought the light of the world flooding around him, and I could hardly believe the difference it made just seeing him, hearing his laugh, pressing my forehead against his. I started bawling because it hit me how the elderly population must feel when loved ones don't come to see them. The thought broke my heart, and I couldn't stop crying as Mike scooped me up and held me in the hospital bed.

"Sweetheart! Sweetheart! What's wrong?"

"I just want to go home. I'm tired of being in these different hospitals. I just want to go home."

They let me out later that afternoon, but before I left, a doctor asked to speak with me. "We took some scans, and your stomach and colon are still pretty inflamed," she said. "We're putting you on some steroids and some high doses of antibiotics, but you'll need to follow up with your oncologist next week."

"Okay." I nodded. "Thank you for everything."

The kids were so excited to hug me that I could hardly believe it. None of them wanted to let me go, and suddenly all the suffering in the world was worth feeling their joy and arms around me.

"Mama, are we gonna keep flipping the coin?" Indy asked. "I wonder where we'll go next. It was so much fun in Bozeman! Mike brought us shopping, and we got fancy food."

I snorted with amusement. I'd been claustrophobic in the hospital, and they'd had the time of their lives. I raised a brow to Mike. "You make even the hardest moments the best of times."

Sky stepped forward. "So do you, Mom!" She hugged me, then grinned at her siblings. "Shopping was pretty cool in Bozeman. We even heard people calling it Boze Angeles. Downtown is a lot different than you'd expect for Montana."

Mike and I met eyes. "It sounds awesome."

"All right, kids," Mike said. "I think we're heading home now. Your mom has had a lot of excitement."

"Hey, Mike, before we leave Montana, can I make a call?" I turned so the kids couldn't see me and whispered, "I still need to talk to the attorney."

"Sure!"

So, Mike and the kids sat in a little picnic area as I called Doug, a man who I'd grown to trust far more than I ever expected.

"There you are!" Doug said. "I've been trying to reach you. I have really big news!"

"Sorry, we're up in Montana with crazy reception."

"The other party wants to drop the case."

I gasped, clutching the phone so tight. "What? You're kidding?"

"It's a long story, but a judge heard about the case and thought it was a bit ridiculous. Word got around that your ex had absolutely no case. You're an amazing mother who's battling cancer. What kind of a man would do this to someone who is battling cancer?"

"Oh, my gosh!" I could hardly breathe.

"Anyway, I sent some emails to his lawyer and told them how your cancerous brain tumor is gone *and* how we have a doctor's note. They realized they have no case, especially since Sky moved back home."

I remained speechless.

"Elisa?"

"I'm here. I'm here!"

"So, rather than throwing away any more money. They want to drop the case. You just need to sign paperwork acknowledging the withdrawal."

"Oh, Doug. This. THIS! Is. Amazing." I breathed so hard, unable to keep an intense relief from ballooning within my chest. "I get to," I cried. "I get to keep my kids?"

"Well, I don't think you were ever going to lose them. But at least you won't have to keep fighting this nonsense — and cancer. Now you can just focus on enjoying time with your husband and children."

"Oh, thank you, Doug! Thank you. I am so beyond happy right now. I don't know what to say."

"I'll email you the paperwork. Just review it and let me know if you have any questions."

"Perfect. Okay! Thanks again — for everything."

I hung up and darted over to Mike. I told him the news, and the stress of a lifetime left his eyes.

Everything looked beautiful then. We cranked up the radio, drove home from Montana to Idaho, and sang at the top of our lungs. Like the doctor said, "It's three steps forward, two steps backward. Progress is progress."

***

"It needs *a lot* of work, but Mike just bought a twenty-five-foot camper for $600." I told my nurse over a virtual appointment, and she just laughed. "He's gonna fix 'er up fast," I said, "so we can bring it on overnight trips for cancer treatments and take the kids to places we could've never gone otherwise."

"I actually think that's a pretty good compromise. You can rest while you travel and stop when you need to." She paused. "You guys are pretty inspiring, you know that? You're just determined to find the best way through this, aren't you? Even if it is in an RV!"

"This one was Mike's idea! As long as I'm breathing, I might as well enjoy life."

The RV has water damage and was pretty well gutted—let's say it has opportunities—but Mike, the kids, and I are so excited to work on it together and then take trips. As I looked at each of their faces today, I realized how close we've really gotten. A year ago, I'm not sure they would've wanted to be stuck in an RV together. Now, it sounds like the best thing ever.

I'll never forget the moments like this that make life worth living. They aren't the huge moments you'd expect, but rather the little ones that build into something so much bigger—proof of a family's love that only grows more even in spite of hardship.

That aside, I can't stop smiling, looking back on this day. Mike's face lit with pure joy when he pulled up with this rickety RV. I hadn't seen him this excited since he landed that plane!

CHAPTER 43
Harvest

Some of us don't realize how much we're blessing people's lives just by sharing our story. That's what happened for me with Shane Jackson.

He wrote through my author page, EC Stilson. "The post involving Blackfoot, Idaho, and your current situation captivated me and has given me strength to carry on. My problems are pretty insignificant in comparison."

I sat drinking a cup of coffee as I read this message, so honored that a stranger had found my page and decided to share his story with me.

"I'm a single father of now a thirteen-year-old," he wrote. "I've raised her since she was two and a half." And as his story continued, I couldn't fathom how my situation could inspire him. Yes, having cancer is scary. But this man has been through so much more than that—and still found a way to avoid regret.

"You've got to beat this!" his closing paragraph stated. "So, get on with it and put this dying bullshit out of your mind because you're not!"

I shared this story with Mike, and we felt so humbled that such a strong man would find anything worthwhile in our story, especially since we've struggled this month and definitely not felt inspirational.

"Elisa, some of your posts lately have left me just not knowing what to say or reply," one of Shane's latest messages said. "I'm hoping for a speedy recovery."

Then, that giver must have been touched by providence, compelled to do an exceptional act of kindness that I truly needed. "I would like to extend an invitation to come experience potato harvest if you have never done so. To me, it's always been a magical experience seeing the crops come in. We're digging potatoes in Pingree. You and your family would be welcome to come out and see potato harvest from the seat of a tractor, if you would like."

I told Mike and the kids. Trey and Indy were especially excited.

We arrived at the field, where we got to ride in different machines and meet Shane in person.

As I sat in the tractor with him, the entire world thrived with magic. I waved to Mike and the kids, who sat in other machines. Watching potatoes freshly birthed from the ground, I saw God's majesty in all of it. And even just glimpsing Shane's view on life and farming is something I'll cherish forever. That is how he's made it through so much with grace.

"You can go ride in the other one now," Shane said, pointing to a machine a few feet away.

After I stepped from the tractor, I placed my hand on the earth and could almost feel its heartbeat. I love fishing because you never know what surprise God has put on your line. Well, that's kind of how farming is too. There's so much hidden under the ground, just waiting for someone to discover its potential.

"Isn't it amazing how the earth can look so dead and void, yet all of those potatoes were waiting just under the surface?" I told Garrett, the driver of the other vehicle, as he loaded potatoes up a large conveyor belt.

"It really is." He beamed. Then, he told me how fun it was seeing the excitement from all of us. "That Indy is a character. And Trey asked great questions."

"Is this what you always wanted to do?" I asked him.

Garrett said he's in medical school but might drop out. "I just don't know," he said.

"What kind of specialty? What kind of doctor?"

"A dermatologist."

I got chills; this was providential too.

Shane had changed my life and said the exact words I needed to hear at the moment I needed to hear them. Maybe I did the same for Garrett. I told him about my melanoma and how it was a dermatologist who found it and gave me a shot at life.

"Time passes. I thought my kids would grow up by the time I was in my early forties. And then I'd do all sorts of things. But look what happened. I'm fighting just to stay alive. Go for your dreams. Don't give up. There's a reason I'm sitting right by you, telling you my story about skin cancer."

After I stepped back to the hardened earth, I knew Garrett would never forget those words, and I thought about the people's lives he might save in the future. People just like me.

So, Wada Farms, who generously let Shane do all of this for us, had Mike, the kids, and me gather potatoes to keep—straight from the ground. We got several boxes of Russet Burbanks and hearts filled to the brim with wonder.

CHAPTER 44
Always More Ink

Ruby begged me to get a tattoo from her. "Come on, Mom. Please? Mike let me tattoo him. You don't even have a tattoo—not even one."

That wasn't completely true. I have tattoos where they've done radiation. It looks like a bizarre constellation on my stomach and back. They used these marks one of the last times I had radiation when they stuffed the lower half of my body, ribcage down, into a bag that they vacuum sealed. I nearly hyperventilated as the bag immobilized me, and techs used the tattooed dots to line up a red target that shone onto my stomach. Then, they turned on the machine and left me there for forty-five minutes.

This therapy is so strong it literally kills cells. No wonder brain radiation caused the worst headaches ever, and back radiation created stomach issues and nausea that brought me down to a frail size one.

"Could you do a mock tattoo?" I asked, shaking off the memory. "Maybe a rainbow feather with the words always more?" I'd been inspired by the hairdresser who told me the story about her tattoo. "We could spend the whole day together."

"Yes! But we'll need to take pictures if it's only temporary. That way I can show it to my clients."

"Deal." I beamed with pride because Ruby is so selfless and supportive. She really is always more than I could've ever hoped for.

We arranged everything, and on Ruby's only day off, she Sharpied a tattoo on my arm so it could be seen while I played the violin. Mike took pictures. I felt so fancy getting worked on in the same chair where she tattoos her clients. And when Ruby shared photos of me on her website, I felt beautiful despite everything I've gone through.

The mock tattoo stayed vibrant much longer than it should have, and thank God it did. The oncologist called the day after I'd hung out with Ruby. As I listened to my doctor, I traced the beautiful design. For some reason, the reality of my situation stunned me almost more than it ever had before. I suddenly wanted to be well, to be healthy, to be able to hike and run. I just wanted the debilitating sickness to end.

I paused, took a breath, and looked at the fake tattoo my oldest daughter had drawn with so much love. The feather shone brightly, and the words "Always more" practically glowed as I studied them. It means there's always more to people's stories than you might guess, more to your future—some surprise to make your life shine even brighter. There's something positive to focus on, even when things appear dim. God brings in the night, but He always ignites the morning. If you dig deep enough, you'll find more strength, courage, and hope. There really is always more... if you just look for it.

"Are you okay? Elisa?" the doctor's voice pulled me from my thoughts.

I cleared my throat. "You already helped me reframe this. I'll be okay."

And just before I could hang up, he said, "Hey, Elisa?"

"Yeah?"

"It was really nice to talk with you. Cancer can be so hard, but the patients... you have such a great way of looking at life."

I subdued a sob that had formed in my throat. "Thank you! That means a lot. Really."

I hung up, looked at the pictures Mike had taken the day before, and smiled. I felt so grateful that life can be awesome despite hardships. I also knew I needed to buckle up for more rounds of treatments. If the good moments really do outweigh the bad, then the opposite of surgeries, radiation, and IV infusions ought to be pretty damn amazing!

CHAPTER 45
The Will to Live

I first met the Olesons over five years ago at a band audition in Blackfoot. I didn't even live in the area, and I shook with nerves. The legendary band leader, Harry, had seen videos of me fiddling, and although I'd talked with him briefly, I'd never played with the band—or even met the members in it.

Regardless, I went and jammed at the Elks Lodge, having no idea what songs were expected or what the band members would think of me. They played country music. I'd been used to Metallica and Offspring!

My fingers searched frantically for the right notes. I thought I'd blown the audition when, miraculously, a couple got up and danced. They were unforgettable, bringing the music to life in such a tangible way. That's when I relaxed, and my fiddle resounded with double-stops and harmonies. I knew then, I'd made it into the band, Rough Stock.

"Who are they?" I asked a woman at another table about the couple dancing.

"The Olesons are one of the most well-known couples in Blackfoot. Justin recently became a county prosecutor. Christie's a nurse and everyone in town loves her."

I didn't know much about Blackfoot other than the Potato Museum. "They seem nice." I was just grateful they'd unknowingly helped me join a band.

Time passed, and I loved every single fiddle gig all across Idaho and Utah, but that alone wouldn't pay the bills. So, the next year I landed a job—in Blackfoot of all places—running a newspaper just a block from the Elks Lodge.

I met so many legends, including people like the Olesons, the Rupes, Marc Carroll (the kind mayor), the Rotary group, American Legion members, people with the Historical Society, those with the senior centers. The list goes on and on. And thousands of *amazing* readers! All these people helped by spreading good things about the paper and providing story tips. The *Morning News* had almost gone under right before I got there, but through everyone's support, we somehow kept that small-town paper running with local news, even if I had to try new things that *really* put me out of my comfort zone.

One day, Justin's awesome brother, Andrew, invited me to inoculate cows.

"Could be a great story," he said, and before I knew it, I headed to his dad's place so we could "get 'er done." Christie artfully showed me how to give the shots while Justin branded the cows. I did pretty great, for a city girl, until I inoculated myself. No one's perfect.

Months later, a large conglomerate broke my heart by buying the newspaper and only keeping one employee for the long haul. I thought the biggest fight of my life had ended, but, if I'd learned anything, it was that life is uncertain.

It was shortly after that when oncologists in Idaho diagnosed me with cancer; they'd found one tumor in my back.

Christie urged me to get a second opinion in Utah. It was a good thing I did. The melanoma team there discovered tumors all up my spine and in my brain. Christie saved my life.

I thought about all of this last week as Justin helped finalize my will. That could've been a sad, emotional thing, especially in my situation, but we smiled and joked. It wasn't until Justin gave me a hefty discount that I really fought to keep the tears at bay. I'd asked him to draft my will because I wanted to somehow pay him and Christie back, yet there he sat, being kind again.

I wondered if the couple really knew how much they've blessed my life from the little things—that first dance and inoculating cows—to the big things like lifesaving advice and drafting my will. Some people might never know what impact they've had.

***

Everyone wants to die well, valiantly, in a way that will make our loved ones proud. I didn't want to be a sniveling person begging to end the pain or crying out for more life.

At the Yom Kippur meeting, they talked about forgiving ourselves and others, about releasing ourselves from vows we'd felt forced to make, or vows we made but could no longer keep. I remembered my New Year's resolution for 2020. "I vow to become as refined as possible," I'd said quietly to myself.

More than a year of hell later, refinement didn't sound quite as romantic. That's a vow I'd like to forget.

When I returned to the synagogue for the second Yom Kippur meeting the next day, I had no idea what to expect, but I knew one thing: It was time to let go of refinement and unattainable goals of perfection.

"God," I prayed during one of the songs, "I get it now. We were never made to be perfect. I might as well be chasing rainbows, trying to reach my self-imposed goals. Can you please just love me, always, as I am? I make more mistakes than anyone I know, but I love you with everything. Please be with me in life and when I die too. I feel ridiculous asking for you to heal me, but please have your will in my life."

I exhaled, feeling oddly lighter than I had in years. And when I opened my eyes, a strange light shone through the synagogue windows.

"*Kadosh. Kadosh. Kadosh.* The whole world is filled with your glory." The music seemed more ancient than time, forged by generations of people who unflinchingly revere God. Given the power of the music and the place itself, maybe it shouldn't be surprising that when I looked down, something surreal unfolded: The sun shot through the glowing stained glass and highlighted specific words on the program I held.

I read the accentuated words. "We are filled with your strength. The strength to bear our afflictions. Add your strength to ours, oh God. So that when death casts its shadow we shall yet be able to say: 'Oh Source of Blessing. You are with us in death as in life.'"

Those words. I can't tell you the power of the words "in death as in life." I knew then God would never abandon me.

A powerful musician stood in front of the congregation and blew the shofar horn with such beautiful resonance that it stunned me. The blast lasted much longer than I'd expected, then went up a fifth and continued until it vibrated me to the core.

I cried right there, my program still illuminated as I shook, my burdens lifted, and my heart full.

Before the "break the fast" celebration, I managed to catch a couple of pictures of my program before the lighting changed too much.

The whole world really is filled with His glory.

CHAPTER 46
Hope

"I don't want to lose my ability to talk and sing," I told Mike while we waited for scan results. The results would determine if I needed radiation on my neck and throat.

"You just need to stay positive," Mike said, even though I'd caught him crying when the kids weren't around, and he thought I'd fallen asleep. My chest physically hurt as I listened to him, knowing he didn't need to know I'd heard my larger-than-life man in the throes of despair. The fear had finally gotten to him. It's the same thing that'd eat me faster than cancer if I let it.

To combat this, I've been attending several different churches that aren't in the same state, not even the same religion. Thanks to Zoom, one church is in Hollywood, one is in New York. I also physically attend a Jewish synagogue as well as a Baptist church in Pocatello. Each initial service shocked me. Thanks to friends, all of these congregations were praying for me. My name ran across display screens and lined bulletins.

It's so humbling. This absolute kindness was hard to fathom. And I figured, why not up my chances, right? The more prayers the better. Last December, I even sent a letter to some Brazilian monks. They didn't respond, but hey, at least I tried.

"I feel like I'm breaking," I told Mike that night. "When is it too much? I just don't know if I can do radiation again. Plus, if I lose my voice, I can't nag you."

Mike chuckled. "Elisa, you should see what's on your nightstand."

I went into our bedroom and found a letter with international stamps on it. With anxious hands, I opened the envelope. After months upon months, the monks had written back — in Portuguese!

It took forever, but I finally typed most of the words into Google Translate. The monks explained that they had done a remote spiritual operation on me a few months back, and that I would see the results soon.

"You will win," the translation read. "Do not be discouraged, persist a little longer. Do not cultivate pessimism. Focus on doing good. Forget the suggestions of destructive fear. Keep going even while avoiding the shadow of your own mistakes. Advance even through tears."

I thought about these kind monks, about my visits to the synagogue, the rainbow on my program, the people I've met, and everything I've learned throughout this whole experience. And as so many thoughts crashed over me like oceanic waves, a surreal understanding sprouted deep in my soul.

This all happened for a reason.

With everything in me, I understood. It was time to fully trust God. It would *all* be okay.

My phone dinged, interrupting my thoughts. The scan results were in. I could read the virtual report or wait to hear directly from the doctor at my next appointment. I clicked "review test results" because patience is a virtue I lack. And as I waited for the file to load, I thought again of all the many blessings and prayers from so many people.

Mike entered the room. "The results are in," I whispered, and he sat down by me.

I read as soon as the words surfaced on my phone. "The tumors remain the same—stable except for the tumor in my neck." My voice shook, not even sounding like my own.

"Yeah?" Mike implored. He leaned forward, waiting for me to respond.

I dropped my phone on the bed and started sobbing. "The tumor in my neck... is shrinking."

We hugged each other so tightly, like we'd never let go.

We still weren't free and clear, but this was a start. Although we had luck with brain radiation, this was the first sign the *infusions* had begun working.

For me, it was the first tangible sign of hope.

BOOK CLUB GUIDE

1. Could you relate to this story on a personal basis?

2. Did this memoir make you feel specific emotions? If so, why?

3. How do you try to remain positive when you're having a hard time? Did the author relay examples that you might find helpful?

4. Do you have any regrets about your past? If so, how can you live without having any regrets in the future?

5. Is there anything you'd like to accomplish in your life that you haven't already? What, and do you have a plan to do so?

6. Did your opinion of this story change as you read? If so, in what way?

7. What's the one thing you will always remember about the author's experiences?

8. If you could talk to the author, what questions would you want to ask her?

9. What was your favorite and least favorite part about this story?

10. Have you read any other memoirs by EC Stilson? How would you compare them to this?

Acknowledgements

First and foremost, I would like to thank my husband, Mike. Without his drive, kindness, and sense of humor, I don't know how I would've carried on in such high spirits. My children (Ruby, Sky, Trey, Indiana, and little Zeke) are truly my inspiration. They've listened to me read numerous parts of this memoir and even helped with ideas that eventually led to the completion of this publication.

My parents, Philip and Ruby Stilson, believe in me despite all reason, and my in-laws, Steve and Maureen Magagna, have graciously let me into their hearts and home so I could have a place to comfortably stay during treatments in Utah—frankly they made even the hardest days fun.

In addition to this, my siblings Julie (Gregg) Laub, Shane (Kazuna) Stilson, Theresa (Jason) Kunzler, and Angela Lupcho are there for me whenever I need them. My aunts, uncles, cousins, nephews, and nieces are so extraordinarily generous with their love and their time (especially Abi Laub who has made numerous trips to Idaho and the hospital to play board games and just cheer me up even at a moment's notice).

Dee Ready—who I've adopted as family—has guided me throughout this entire process and helped me whenever I've had questions. Her expertise has buoyed me through this experience more than she might know. My good friend, Ralph Hauser, has a sixth sense when it comes to fish *and* people, and he always seems to stop by or send letters when I need encouragement the most. To Scott and Colleen Hancock for their goodness and banana bread, as well as to Kim and Gloria Hansen, Natalie and Terry Bergevin, Jennifer and Jared Grover, Harry and Patsy Sherman, Lisa and Jim Workman (both Jims — actually, the whole Workman family), Kristine Murray, Laurie Allen, Emily Thornton, Kara Saunders, Candiss West, Nicole Nauman, Katy Williams, Donna Bergman, and Inger Wiltz — your love and generosity have moved mountains in my life. I adore all of you.

I'm also extremely grateful to my editor, Robb Grindstaff. He made this memoir what I hoped it would be. Plus, now I can tell people I've personally learned from a legend of the newspaper industry. Kris Norris did a fantastic job on the cover, and I'll always be grateful for how fun she made that process. My publishing team at Evolved Publishing — especially Dave Lane (AKA Lane Diamond) — worked tirelessly, offering time and so much kindness. I'll be forever grateful that you took a chance on this memoir.

And last but not least, thank you to all of my extended family and friends for their support. Without that kindness — including the many comments on my social media channels — I never would've succeeded in completing this project. I am the luckiest.

About the Author

EC Stilson has authored ten novels, and three of her memoirs, in THE GOLDEN SKY TRILOGY, have become No. 1 bestsellers on Amazon for women's memoir. Since 2011, through her writing, fundraisers, book donations, and national radio interviews, EC Stilson has helped raise thousands of dollars for organizations such as Angel Watch, the Pregnancy Resource Center, the American Diabetes Association, and Primary Children's Hospital. When she's not working as an editor, parenting, fiddling, or writing, she is speaking at events or encouraging families at infant loss support groups.

For more, please visit [Author Name] online at:
Website: www.ecwrites.blogspot.com
Goodreads: EC Stilson
Twitter: @ECWrites
Facebook: @AuthorECStilson
Instagram: @ECStilson